Laura Nyro:
LYRICS & REMINISCENCES

Laura's original handwritten lyrics and notes courtesy of the estate of Laura Nyro
Please visit Laura Nyro's website at *www.lauranyro.com*

Cover Design by Smay Vision
Interior Design by Scott Brandsgaard
Adger Cowans' Photography appears on the front cover, page 5, and page 200

Cherry Lane Music:
Manager of Publications/Project Editor: Rebecca Quigley
Director of Publications: Mark Phillips
Interviews and quotes compiled by John Stix
Also available: *Time and Love: The Art & Soul of Laura Nyro* (02500425)

ISBN 1-57560-648-8

In conversations with me, many times Laura referred to herself as a poet. *Laura Nyro: Lyrics and Reminiscences* is essentially a volume of poetry, Laura's words without music. With this in mind, I wish to thank the people who have helped to create this tribute to her life's work.

I am awestruck by Rickie Lee Jones because she so clearly captured the essence of Laura through the flow of her words, her imagery, and her choice of subject matter. That they had never met is of no consequence whatsoever, for it is clear that they shared much on a deeper level, the souls of kindred spirits.

I'm grateful for the generosity of Laura's friends, personal and professional, who took the care and the time to share with us their memories of her within these pages, all of which help to describe Laura's complex and beautiful nature.

To Adger Cowans, I say thank you for having taken such stunning photos of Laura throughout the years. In looking at them, I know that Laura was relaxed in working with you and, therefore, so much of her inner self is visible to all of us.

And to Cherry Lane Music Publishing, for sparking this project and for seeing it through, I wish to express my admiration as well as my deep appreciation.

Patty DiLauria

Patricia DiLauria, Laura and Maria's Friend

FOREWORD

Laura Nyro is a part of the template from which my own musical and Feminine consciousness was printed. In the back of my mind, I knew Laura had done it, even before I was sure what "It" was. It turns out that "It" meant making no apologies, not being a victim, celebrating the voice and exploring how the voice connected to being a woman in the real world. She has done a lot of work for us, as a matriarch, as a singer and songwriter, to make sure we are more comfortable in our own authority, to encourage and defend, to give us permission. Thank you, Laura. It would have been a lot harder without you.

Rosanne Cash

INTRODUCTION

Up in the sky there are a thousand stars we might see in our lifetime. Circuses circling fathoms of infinite seas, in dimensions we will never catch in the corner of our eye, on great caravans of reflected light and hope. I once saw a painting called *The Equestrian in the Circus of the Falling Star*. That is where I see Laura Nyro now, where I keep her, where she can work and be as wild as she is.

The teenaged genius, she runs through subways unharmed by the bad people who hide there, and she never grows old. Eroticism; she's there like Joan of Arc. No pseudo sex queen could even approach the sensuality Laura brought with a couple chords and a Chinese lamp. Let the boys and girls grow their own new sexuality from the intoxicating leaves of these times, these hippies and greasers and soci's.

Courageous revolutionary, white women singing about her, about our Black Panther brothers—that was the big surprise. She had me swooning for a lover up her stairs, angry at my boyfriend tomcat, and then she gave me a gun and said, "Are we going to leave our heroes here to die?" I was thinking, "Well, they aren't my heroes, but I'll wait here till I learn what I am not seeing now."

These things are true of her, but there is something greater maybe, something we all have, the first thing that makes the other things resound so gloriously. I suspect it was just the girl she was. Ultimately, just a girl—somebody's daughter, sister, mother, girlfriend.

I never met her, except through her music. It's not that I think about her much in these years; I don't. But I don't need to. Mythological creatures are part of us. And I suspect it is the metaphysical clay of her intention that I work with.

So there she is, horse bound, twirling in the cosmos, made of the purple lipstick that only defiant tenderness can bear. All that color, all that eternal burning, all that practice after school.

Against the backdrop of that time, perhaps nothing less than genius after all—genius being a thing that resonates deeper than its time, that cannot be denied by its creator, that, measured against the time, was a courageous and unexpected use of tools; and measured against history, has no relevance to any time but now. The pretty folk singers and the angry acid queens, the guitar slingers and the soul groups, none of it translated with its original power into the coming decades. But this artist is still intact, and when you listen to those old recordings, you cannot help but hear the voice, like any great voice, Miles or Kubrick or Dylan Thomas, not only a great decade, but a great soul. Laura Nyro, songwriter and singer.

And this is the gift, you know, inspired from within. It is not what she did but what she was. Where I can discern the truly divine among us, those brushed for a moment by God's little watercolor. What they do is amazing, yes, but it is because of what they are that the work is profound.

Why is "Upstairs by a Chinese Lamp" such an amazing work? Because it is being generated by a spirit wholly bent on love, on bringing love to the listener. I believe that now. I knew the song; it made me dream and made me hope. But now, growing old, I see that the intention of the writer was the thing that made the song live. In performance, the writer tells us many layers more than the music or the lyric can. If the writer is a performer, a great interpreter, like Laura, the inflection and movement reveal that meaning that cannot be spoken, but is understood by most of the people who witness it. Writers, critics, can try to tell you about it, but it is not a thing that can really be told or understood intellectually. It just doesn't matter much that way. Simply closing her eyes, we knew that this song was the banner of a noble and courageous character, a very, very sexually compelling image, driven not by beauty but by loneliness—a loneliness that made her beautiful. We get that watching her go inward. I actually never saw that, but I felt it each time I heard the song.

We who were a little homely or a little stunningly beautiful for our oddness were proud of our having been cool enough to have heard her. Most people did not know who she was, and recognition of this secret in common, this was a bond between strangers. My first co-writer, we met out on the boardwalk in Venice, and we were friends right away, largely in part because he could play, and I could sing, Laura Nyro songs.

I first saw her on PBS back in 1969 or '70. I was captivated and, well, repelled at the same time. I wondered what the heck had happened to her? She was so...sad and dark, so filled with self. She was like a trailer park gone out driving by itself. She looked like an autistic child then, unable to look up, contorting, consumed by the song she sang. It seemed a bit much, and yet absolutely real, and I was spellbound.

At that same time I read about her in a magazine in a high school library where I spent my work study time. Janis Ian mentioned her as the greatest songwriter around. I had loved her "Society's Child," and so I was curious about Laura. I liked her name, and that she was from New York City, that strange other world, where *West Side Story* came from. Living on a farm in Elma, Washington, a small town where I was outcast absolute, it helped me to survive just knowing that somewhere in the universe there was someone with that beautiful name, Laura Nyro, and people cared about her, and there was a city where she walked and the wind lifted her hair.

The wind lifted her hair for some magical moment on the cover of *New York Tendaberry*, my first Laura record, and for me, her greatest work. She was not afraid to show you her strange face, and you could tell she felt very comfortable with her body. Something as small as that, something as simple as "Look at me, I am different, see me" can be ingested instantly and change you in a small way, a way that one day might become very large indeed. All of these simple gestures we do seep into and carve the people we meet. Every photograph, every thing, it is part of telling people who we are, part of the great word of God that we speak.

The years passed, the times changed, the Panthers died away, if not in body in spirit. I wish we had come further than we have in our civil rights for all people in America. We seemed to be heading forward so well, and then, as if by purposeful annihilation through some horrifying edification of our symbols, it all just was consumed by media. And then it was gone.

The great black leaders became little more than great hairstyles, caricaturized on TV shows as pimps and ne'er-do-wells, and the black women on television went from house servants to the ladies of the houses with the servants, as if somehow that made it better. Watching the movement of black people consumed by white TV and then ridiculed, seeing many things cool out on the street, many prejudices fade in my own lifetime, it is harrowing to watch what is going on now.

Now a seedy thread of contempt can be felt on airwaves dominated by white men in suits—contempt for women, contempt for other races, contempt for any idea that is not their own. I see it every day on Fox programming. Sorry to mention a TV station, one that will one day fade away, but as of this writing, they are the perpetrators of some very, very bad behavior in our once civil and just conversations. There are a whole bunch of white people who are still shifting nervously when black people sit in the desk next to them, and still snickering at beautiful female bodies. Snickering on the air!

But the threads of dignity for all people, embracing the concept that white man cannot rule other people, are strong, and they will not be broken. As of this writing, much is being done to undo the work so many fought for in the '60s and '70s; it is. The rights of human beings are being trampled again. Women lost a simple equal rights amendment, and we are all in danger of losing much more than we have ever lost before: the right to live and speak and fight against a government we do not believe in.

And while the black community has been chopped up and sold back to itself in the shape of million dollar pimps, child prostitute singers, and murderers with record contracts, there is still this thread among many great musicians of music directed toward teaching, toward healing, toward bring about dignity and unity. Dignity is hard to come by in any language, but the language of despair is still sung loudly in our country. There are still people angry about laws aimed at establishing an equal playing field. A human being's experience is not a group experience. It is not about our color. But our color must never be a point of shame or humiliation. And as subtle as a song, these concepts are being perpetrated subtly and not so subtly once again.

There is still a lot to sing and write about, to heal the spirit and encourage the revolution among our people. Poverty in the United States in this new millennium is a sin that more than one President will have to account for when his time is up. Laura Nyro inspires that kind of thinking in me. I want to stand by the people in my nation and help us all rise. I can't say how, I only know that these songs, these songs of freedom, and their writers, are my teachers and companions.

Toward the end of her career, and her life, Laura retired to a more personal statement. She focused on animals and children, my favorite subjects as well, and she lived in Connecticut with her close friend, Maria, and raised a son, Gil, and these were the people she devoted her days and nights to. And for a while then, wrote songs standing at some distance from the churning fireball of the music business. She popped up now and then on some stage somewhere in New York, but for the most part, music business was no longer her business.

I had the honor of singing at the Beacon Theater in a memorial for her a few months after she died. It was there that I met some of the people who knew her, and learned (though I had suspected) that she liked my work quite a lot. Singing her songs in public had been something I had always imagined doing, had sung in my room since I was sixteen, and it came quite easily to me. I must say now it was one of the greatest moments I have known onstage. It was a great night, and don't we all wish we could be at our own memorials before we fly to heaven. We would be very pleased, indeed.

I know that she was.

Rickie Lee Jones
July 2003
The Beach, Los Angeles, CA

Contents

**17 More Than a New Discovery (1967)
The First Songs (1973)**

19 Wedding Bell Blues

21 Billy's Blues

23 California Shoeshine Boys

25 Blowin' Away

27 Lazy Susan

28 Goodbye Joe

29 Flim Flam Man

31 Stoney End

32 I Never Meant to Hurt You

33 He's a Runner

34 Buy and Sell

37 And When I Die

39 Eli and the Thirteenth Confession (1968)

41 Lucky

43 Lu

45 Sweet Blindness

47 Poverty Train

48 Lonely Women

50 Eli's Comin'

51 Timer

54 Stoned Soul Picnic (Picnic, A Green City)

57 Emmie

59 Woman's Blues

61 Once It Was Alright Now (Farmer Joe)

63 December Boudoir

66 The Confession

69 New York Tendaberry (1969)

71 You Don't Love Me When I Cry

73 Captain for Dark Mornings

74 Tom Cat Goodbye

75 Mercy on Broadway

77 Save the Country

78 Gibsom Street

80 Time and Love

81 Man Who Sends Me Home

82 Sweet Lovin' Baby

83 Captain Saint Lucifer

85 New York Tendaberry

87 Christmas and the Beads of Sweat (1970)

88 Brown Earth

90 When I Was a Freeport and You Were the Main Drag

91 Blackpatch

92 Been on a Train

93 Upstairs by a Chinese Lamp

96 Map to the Treasure

97 Beads of Sweat

99 Christmas in My Soul

101 Smile (1976)

102 Children of the Junks

103 Money

105 I Am the Blues

106 Stormy Love

107 Cat Song

109 Midnite Blue

110 Smile

113 Season of Lights (1977)

114 Morning News

117 Nested (1978)

119 Mr. Blue (The Song of Communications)

121 Rhythm and Blues

124 My Innocence

126 Crazy Love

127 American Dreamer

128 Springblown

129 Sweet Sky

130 Light-Pop's Principle

133 Child in a Universe

134 Nest

135 Wind Circles

137 Mother's Spiritual (1984)

139 To a Child

141 The Right to Vote

142 A Wilderness

144 Melody in the Sky
145 Late for Love
147 Free Thinker
148 Man in the Moon
149 Talk to a Green Tree
150 Trees of the Ages
151 The Brighter Song
152 Roadnotes
153 Sophia
155 Mother's Spiritual
156 Refrain

159 Live at the Bottom Line (1990)
160 Roll of the Ocean
161 Companion
162 Wild World
163 Park Song
166 Broken Rainbow
167 Dancers Sweepers Bookkeepers (Women of the One World)
170 Japanese Restaurant

173 Walk the Dog and Light the Light (1993)
175 A Woman of the World
177 The Descent of Luna Rose
179 Art of Love
180 Lite a Flame
181 Louise's Church
183 Walk the Dog and Light the Light

185 Angel in the Dark (2001)
186 Angel in the Dark
187 Triple Goddess Twilight
189 Sweet Dream Fade
190 Serious Playground
191 Gardenia Talk
192 Animal Grace
193 Don't Hurt Child
194 CODA

Song lyrics

More Than A New Discovery (1966)

The First Songs (1973)

Wedding Bell Blues
Bill I love you so
I always will
I look at you and see
The passion eyes of May
Oh but am I ever
Gonna see my wedding day?

Oh I was on your side Bill
When you were loosin'
I'd never scheme or lie Bill
There's been no foolin'
But kisses and love
Won't carry me
'Til you marry me Bill

I love you so
I always will.
And in your voice
I hear a choir of carosels
Oh but am I ever
Gonna hear my wedding bells?

I was the one came runnin'
When you were lonely
I haven't lived a day
Not lovin' you only
But kisses and love
Won't carry me
Til you marry me Bill
I got the wedding bell blues
Marry me Bill
I got the wedding bell blues

Wedding Bell Blues

Bill
I love you so
I always will
I look at you and see
The passion eyes of May
Oh but am I ever gonna see
My wedding day?
Oh I was on your side Bill
When you were losin'
I'd never scheme or lie Bill
There's been no foolin'
But kisses and love won't
    carry me
Till you marry me Bill
Bill
I love you so
I always will
And in your voice I hear
A choir of carousels
Oh but am I ever gonna hear
My wedding bells?
I was the one came runnin'
When you were lonely
I haven't lived one day
Not loving you only
But kisses and love won't
    carry me
Till you marry me Bill

Bill
I love you so
I always will
And though devotion rules my
    heart
I take no bows

Oh but Bill you know
I wanna take my wedding vows
Come on Bill
Come on Bill
I got the wedding bell blues

When MGM gave us the budget, it was not big. I could use some strings on three or four sides. It forced me to be really creative and go in with piano, bass, and drums. My model was Peggy Lee's "Black Coffee" album. I went in with Toots Thielman on harmonica, Jay Berliner on guitar, and Stan Free on piano. I used an alto and bass flute and a cello. On "Billy's Blues" I used a bluesy trumpet thing right out of a smoky nightclub. This is something no one knows. Maybe Milt [Okun, producer, *The First Songs*]. When we mixed "Billy's Blues," at the end there is a chime. I love it. The chime fades. When they cut the tape or pressed the album they cut that chime off. Every time I hear that I get so mad. I go, "Where is that god-dammed chime!"

—HERB BERNSTEIN, ARRANGER, *THE FIRST SONGS*

Billy's Blues

Billy's blue
With his head hangin' to
His shoes
Right the wrong
Or play a song
To ease Billy's blues

Billy's down
He was born he was bound
To lose
Right the wrong
Or play a song
To ease Billy's blues

Some folks have it good
And some folks have it no good
But Billy's got it bad
He's so endlessly sad

Billy's blue
With his head hangin' to
His shoes
Somebody please right the wrong
Or play a song
To ease Billy's blues

To ease Billy's blues

She used to play all the time for her friends. She loved to sit down when it was just the family and play for a half hour. She would play some of the old rock 'n' roll songs she never recorded. "O-o-h Child." She would do the older ones; she started in the subways singing songs from the '50s. Those were in her private repertoire. She used to do "Cowboys to Girls." I remember when we used to play shoot 'em up, bang, bang, baby.

—ELLEN URYEVICK, FRIEND, HARPIST IN HARPBEAT

California Shoeshine Boys

California shoeshine boys
Countin' up their dimes
Countin' up the girls they've known
And countin' up the times
I got heartache
But I got news
California shoeshine boys
You can shine my shoes

California shoeshine boys
Never really care
Only for that California shoeshine
In their hair
I got heartache
But I got news
California shoeshine boys
You can shine my shoes

California shoeshine boys
Rappin' ten feet tall
John can make sweet Cindy cry
But Joe can make her crawl
I got heartache
But I got news
California shoeshine boys
You can shine my shoes

She would listen to less then you might think. She never listened to a lot of radio at all. She would have a few cassettes. She loved old rock-and-roll, the doo-wop stuff.

—ROSCOE HARRING, LAURA'S SOUND ENGINEER, ROAD MANAGER

Blowin' Away

You ole fire
I'm mad with desire
You're my favorite one
Got me cookin' like a fever
Got my love runnin' for the sun
I feel so high
I feel like I may
Go blowin' away

My well meaner
My day fancy dreamer
Oh what can it be?
Well it's something like a power
Like a hold and it's holdin' me
I feel so high
I feel like I may
Go blowin' away

My long laster
My soft hearted master
Ain't been born and bred
But he's standin' in my doorway
In my mind
Up above my head
I feel so high
I feel like I may
Go blowin' away

I met her when I was 19. I liked the first record. Then I heard *Eli and the Thirteenth Confession* and got obsessed with it. My manager had a lot of contacts and arranged for me to meet her. I essentially went to her apartment in New York City when she still lived there and met her. She made tuna fish casserole. In fact, it was the only thing she knew how to make. It was the reason her publishing company was called Tuna Fish Music. I remember she tried to get me to sing along or play along with her on these classic R&B tunes. Some of them I just didn't know the words. Also, I was really embarrassed about singing in front of her, singing along with her even. At the time I wasn't a singer at all. I wrote all the songs but I had resigned myself to just singing backgrounds. Some weeks later she called me up and asked me if I wanted to become a bandleader for her. At the time I was in the Nazz and as much as the opportunity tortured me because of my admiration for her, I couldn't just simply leave the band and become a bandleader for Laura Nyro.

—TODD RUNDGREN, ARTIST, FAN, AND PRODUCER

Lazy Susan

Lazy flower
My you've grown so tall
I have lost
And loved him
You have seen it all

Lazy Susan
Lazy thru
Hasn't got a thing to do
Oh but to sit there
And light up the hillside
Sun fried
Black-eyed Sue

Lazy Susan
Lazy thru
All the hills in love with you
Courted and cradled
By heaven and hillside
Sun fried
Black-eyed Sue
Black-eyed

Black-eyed Sue
How happy you must be
Once I too
Had someone lovin' me

Johnny Johnny
Warm and true
That's how I remember you
This morning
Just as I found you
Up there on the hillside

With sun fried
Blackeyed lazy Susan

Goodbye Joe

We were lost in the fair
On the highland
Goodbye Joe
With the sky and the deer
On the highland

Goodbye Joe
Time is full of changes
And now you've got to go
Don't forget that we loved
On the highland
Goodbye Joe

Goodbye Joe
Yes I understand
I'm trying not to cry
But if I do
It's only 'cause I'll miss you
One last time let me kiss you

I remember
When you came a calling
Goodbye Joe
Like a sunrise
That rose without warning

Goodbye Joe
Time is full of changes
And now you've got to go
And we walked
On a Manhattan morning
Goodbye Joe

Film Flam Man

Hands off the man
The flim flam man
His mind is up his sleeve
And his talk is make believe
Oh lord
The man's a fraud
He's a flim flam man

Hands off the man
The flim flam man
He's the one in the Trojan horse
Making out like he's Santa Claus
Oh lord
The man's a fraud
He's a flim flam man
He's a fox
He's a flim flam man

Everybody wants him
The people and the police
And all the pretty ladies disarm
The beautiful gent
You know he has hardly a cent
He pays his monthly rent
With daily charm

Hands off the man
The flim flam man
His mind is up his sleeve
And his talk is make believe
Oh lord
The man's a fraud
He's a flim flam man
He's so cagey
He's an artist

He's a fox
He's a flim flam man
Don't believe
Him he's a flim flam
Ole road runner

I was hired by her manager and publisher, Artie Mogul and Paul Barry. They hired me to produce an album. They brought her up to the studio and I listened to her sing. I think she was 18. I was taken with her voice, her lyrics, and her melodies. I was taken with her singing and piano playing.

—MILT OKUN, PRODUCER, *THE FIRST SONGS*

Stoney End

I was born from love
And my poor mother worked the mines
I was raised on the good book Jesus
'Til I read between the lines
Now I don't believe I wanna see the morning
Going down the stoney end
I never wanted to go down the stoney end
Mama let me start all over
Cradle me
Mama cradle me again

I can still remember him
With lovelight in his eyes
But the light flickered out and parted
As the sun began to rise
Now I don't believe I wanna see the morning
Going down the stoney end
I never wanted to go down the stoney end
Mama let me start all over
Cradle me
Mama cradle me again

Never mind the forecast
'Cause the sky has lost control
'Cause the fury and the broken thunder's
Come to match my ragin' soul
Now I don't believe I wanna see the morning
Going down the stoney end
I never wanted to go down the stoney end
Mama let me start all over
Cradle me
Mama cradle me again.

I Never Meant to Hurt You

I never meant to hurt you
I'm not that way at all
Please believe the words of a heart
A heart that seems so small

I never meant to hurt you
I guess I lost my place
Please believe the words of a heart
A heart that hides its face

Why do I do things
I never mean to do?
Why did I speak so carelessly
When all that I felt was love for you

And I swear
I never meant to hurt you
I've got to make you know
Please believe the words of a heart
A heart that didn't show

I never meant to hurt you
I only meant to love you it's true
And when I saw you crying
I cried too

He's a Runner

He's a runner
And he'll run away
Soon there'll be no man
Woman ain't been born who can make him stay
Woman get away while you can

He's a runner
And he'll run away
With the midnight train
Woman ain't been born who can make him stay
Come the judgment day, come the rain
He's a runner

There'll come the runnin'
He'll know he's got to
Don't ask him not to or why
Oh why on why did you leave me
And run off with tomorrow?
Now I'm in chains
Till I die

He's a runner
And he'll run away
Soon there'll be no man
Woman ain't been born who can make him stay
Woman get away while you can
He's a runner
He's a runner
And he's got to run away

Buy and Sell

Cocaine and quiet beers
Sweet candy and caramel
Pass the time and dry the tears
On a street called buy and sell

Life turns like the endless sea
Death tolls like a vesper bell
Children laugh and lovers dream
On a street called buy and sell

Ladies dress calico style
Beware your heart
When they smile
And their men walk shamelessly
Aimlessly by
Cinders in the daylight
Junkyards in the sky

Buy and sell
Sell my goods to buy my roof
My bed
Two pennies will buy a rose
Three pennies and who can tell?
On a street
That comes and goes
By the name of buy and sell

Sell my goods to buy my roof
My bed

There were no tracks, no lead sheets; there was nothing. There was Milt Okun standing there, there was Laura, and there was me. And she sat at the piano and played me some of the songs. I put a lead sheet together and Milt put the arrangement together. She knew what she wanted. I was sort of the devil's advocate. She had this raw talent which was wonderful. I just tried to embellish what she was doing. Truthfully; the ideas were hers: "Flim Flam Man," "Wedding Bell Blues," "And When I Die," "Stoney End." She had that feel. I had to capture on record what she was laying down. It was tricky because I didn't want to bastardize what she was doing. I tried to keep the wonderful stuff she was doing and not let it get too off the path.

—HERB BERNSTEIN, ARRANGER, *THE FIRST SONGS*

Stoned
Surry d
To a st
Surry o
To a s
There'll
Red yel
Sassafr
Stoned

There'
There
There
Train
Com
On s

Can
Can
Sum
To
Rai
And
Co
su

And when I die

I

I'm not scared of dyin'
And I don't really care
If it's peace you find in dyin'
Well then let the time be near
If it's peace you find in dyin'
When dyin' time is here
Just bundle up my coffin
'Cause it's cold way down there
And when I die
And when I'm gone
There'll be one child born
And a world to carry on

II

My troubles are many
They're as deep as a well
I swear there aint no heaven
And pray there aint no hell
Swear there aint no heaven
And pray their aint no hell
But I'll never know by livin'
Only my dyin will tell
And when I die
And when I'm gone
There'll be one child born
And a world to carry on

III

Give me my freedom
For as long as I be
All I ask of livin'
Is to have no chains on me
All I ask of livin'
Is to have no chains on me
And ~~all ask~~ when I die
And when I'm gone
There'll be one child born
And a world to carry on

There'll be one child born
And a world to carry on
Carry on ___

And When I Die

I'm not scared of dyin'
And I don't really care
If it's peace you find in dyin'
Well then let the time be near
If it's peace you find in dyin'
When dyin' time is here
Just bundle up my coffin
'Cause it's cold way down there

And when I die
And when I'm gone
There'll be one child born
And a world to carry on

My troubles are many
They're as deep as a well
I swear there ain't no heaven
And I pray there ain't no hell
Swear there ain't no heaven
And pray there ain't no hell
But I'll never know by livin'
Only my dyin' will tell

And when I die
And when I'm gone
There'll be one child born
And a world to carry on

Give me my freedom
For as long as I be
All I ask of livin'
Is to have no chains on me
All I ask of livin'
Is to have no chains on me
And all I ask of dyin'

Is to go naturally

And when I die
And when I'm gone
There'll be one child born
And a world to carry on

Eli And The Thirteenth Confession (1968)

Eli and the Thirteenth Confession changed my life. That record blew the doors off. The thing about Laura for me was her poetry and her passion and her femininity, her feminism. She was distilling a number of styles that she made her own, including Motown, street corner doo-wop, jazz, Broadway, and a poetic lyric sensibility. I also think that *Eli* was groundbreaking on an arrangement level for a pop record, for those kinds of orchestrations.

—PETER GALLWAY, ARTIST, PRODUCER, *TIME AND LOVE: THE MUSIC OF LAURA NYRO*
(TRIBUTE ALBUM)

Lucky

Yes I'm ready
So come on Luckie
Well there's an avenue
Of Devil who
Believe in stone
You can meet
The Captain
At the dead end zone
What Devil doesn't know
Is that Devil can't stay
Doesn't know he's seen his day
Oh Luckie's takin' over
And his clover shows
Devil can't get out of hand
'Cause Luckie's takin' over
And what Luckie says goes
Dig them potatoes
If you never dug your girl before
Poor little Devil he's a backseat
    man to Luckie
Forever more!

Yes I'm ready
So come on Luckie
Luckie
Inside of me
Inside of my mind
Inside of my mind
Don't go fallin' for Naughty
Don't go fallin' for Naughty
He's a dragon
With a double bite
Sure can do his short changin'
Out a sight
An artist of a sort

But a little bit short of luck
This lucky night
Oh Luckie's takin' over
And his clover shows
Naughty can't get out of hand
'Cause Luckie's takin' over
And what Luckie says
Goes
Dig them potatoes
If you never dug your girl before
Poor little naughty
He's a backseat man to Luckie
    forever
A backseat man to Luckie
Hey! Hey! Hey!
It's a real good day to go get
    Luckie

She was into jazz and R&B and many different styles of music. She was an eclectic writer. With the songs that she had written, one of them would sound like jazz. So I would say, "Listen to this," and play her Art Blakey and the Jazz Messengers. I'd say, "Listen to the instrumentation; this is only trumpet and tenor sax." She would say, "Yeah, this would work." The introduction to "Lu" actually laid down the feeling of what she was going to do. One of the things she did that was unique was to play chords differently than anybody else I ever worked with. I used this technique I learned from her throughout my career. She actually learned how to play by using the upper parts of the chords. Most musicians, when they play chords, play basic chords, like C to F to G. What Laura did was play a Cmaj9 without the 3rd—a G major chord with the C in the bass. She would play triads but she would play the "wrong" bass notes, which would make the chords sound unusual. By doing that it altered the sound of the way she wrote her songs. All through her life she played that style. I used that technique on a lot of hit records and no one realized that I got it from Laura. Other composers tried to imitate her and tried to utilize that style. Basically, they were not able to get the thing emotionally the way she was able to.

—CHARLIE CALLELO, PRODUCER, *ELI AND THE THIRTEENTH CONFESSION*

Lu

Silver was the color
Winter was a snowbell
Mother of the windboys
Livin' off the lovewell
I was livin' off the lovewell
Lovewell
With Lu
And everybody's callin' Luie
Luie Luie
You got a thing about you
Keep the light goin' for Luie
And Luie keeps on pushin' thru

Thru
Keeps on pushin'
Amber was the color
Summer was a flameride
Cookin' up the noon roads
Walkin' on God's good side
I was walkin' on God's good side
God's good side
With Lu
And everybody's callin' Luie
Luie Luie
You got a thing about you
Keep the light goin' for Luie
And Luie keeps on pushin' thru
Thru
Keeps on pushin' thru
Thru
He keeps on pushin'
I will always be fair
Be there
For Lu
Forever and ever more

Everybody
Everybody everybody
Yeah! Yeah! Yeah!
And everybody's callin' Luie
Callin' Luie
Everybody's callin' Luie
Callin'
My man
My man Luie
Callin' Luie
My man Luie
Callin' Luie
My man Luie
Callin' Luie
Luie
People and the captain
Callin' my man Luie

When we recorded "Sweet Blindness," we did it the same day we did "Lucky" and "Lu," I believe. "Sweet Blindness" was her actual definition of what it was like to get drunk; what it was like to be blind in a sense that it was sweet in a way that alcohol had a tendency to make you feel. She wrote the *Eli* record and the various trilogies within it with specific points of view. Although I discussed what the songs were about, in her brain I think they were sort of like impressionistic paintings of experiences rather than [her] actually trying to get them to make sense.

—CHARLIE CALLELO, PRODUCER, *ELI AND THE THIRTEENTH CONFESSION*

Sweet Blindness

Down by the grapevine
Drink my daddy's wine
Get happy
Down by the grapevine
Drink my daddy's wine
Get happy
Happy!

Oh sweet blindness
A little magic
A little kindness
Oh sweet blindness
All over me
Four leaves on a clover
I'm just a bit of a shade
    hungover
Come on baby do a slow float
You're a good lookin' riverboat
And ain't that sweet-eyed
    blindness
Good to me
Down by the grapevine
Drink my daddy's wine
Good mornin'
Down by the grapevine
Drink my daddy's wine
Good mornin'
Mornin'!
Oh sweet blindness
A little magic
A little kindness
Oh sweet blindness
All over me
Please don't tell my mother

I'm a saloon and a moonshine
    lover
Come on baby do a slow float
You're a good lookin riverboat
And ain't that sweet-eyed
    blindness
Good to me
(Don't ask me 'cause I)
Ain't gonna tell you
What I've been drinkin'
Ain't gonna tell you
What I've been drinkin'
Ain't gonna tell you
What I've been drinkin'
Wine
Of wonder
Wonder!
(By the way)
Sweet blindness
A little magic
A little kindness
Oh sweet blindness
All over me
Don't let daddy hear it
He don't believe in the gin mill
    spirit
Come on baby do a slow float
You're a good lookin' riverboat
And ain't that sweet-eyed
    blindness
Good to me
Good to me
Now ain't that sweet-eyed
    blindness
Good to me

She was kind of forced to immerse herself in performance a bit more than if she had been given all the time in the world to just do it whenever it came out. Because of the success of that album [*Eli and the Thirteenth Confession*] she did gain greater freedom but on no record that she made after that did she achieve the same level of intensity.

—**TODD RUNDGREN, ARTIST, FAN AND PRODUCER**

Poverty Train

Last call for the poverty train
Last call for the poverty train
It looks good and dirty
On Shiny light strip
And if you don't get beat
You got yourself a trip

You can see the walls roar
See your brains on the floor
Become God
Become cripple
Become funky
And split
Why was I born

I just saw the Devil
And he's smilin' at me
I heard my bones cry
"Devil why's it got to be"
Devil played with my brother
Devil drove my mother
Now the tears in the gutter
Are floodin' the sea
Why was I born

Oh baby
It looks good and dirty
Them shiny lights glow
A million night tramps
Tricks and tracks
Will come and go
You're starvin' today
But who cares anyway
Baby it feels like I'm dyin'

Now
I swear there's somethin' better
    than
Getting off on sweet cocaine
It feels so good
It feels so good
Getting off the poverty train
Mornin'

Lonely Women

No one hurries home
To lonely women
No one hurries home
To lonely women
A gal could die without her man
And no one knows it better than
Lonely women

No one knows the blues
Like lonely women do
No one knows the blues
Like lonely women
Blues that make the walls rush in
Walls that tell you where you've been
And you've been to the hollow
Lonely women

Let me die
Early mornin'
Whoa whoa whoa bitter tears
Whoa whoa whoa bitter tears
Uptight
Downpour
Don't got no children
To be grandmother for
Grandmother for
She don't believe no more
She don't believe
No one hurries home to call you baby
Everybody knows
Everybody knows
Everybody
Knows
But no one knows

She stood in front of the band and sang live on "Eli's Comin'." We did eventually overdub it, but she sang live and it was a very inspiring session. Of course, in those days we did the horns and rhythm live because we were limited in tracks. I don't remember how long it took us, but it may have taken a couple of days. It was done on 4-track.

—**CHARLIE CALLELO, PRODUCER,** *ELI AND THE THIRTEENTH CONFESSION*

Eli's Comin'

Eli's comin'
Eli's a comin'
Whoa you better hide your heart
Your lovin' heart
Eli's a comin' and the cards say
Broken heart
Oh broken heart
Eli's comin'
Hide your heart girl
Eli's comin'
Hide your heart girl
Girl
Eli's a comin'
Better hide
Girl
Eli's a comin'
Better hide your heart
Your heart
Eli's comin'
Hide your heart
You better better hide your heart
Eli's comin' better walk
Walk but you'll never get away
Never get away from the burn
And the heartache
I walked
To Apollo and the bay
And everywhere I go
Eli's a comin'
Eli's a comin'
Eli's a comin' and he's comin'
To get me mama
I'm down on my knees
Eli's comin'
Hide it

Girl
Eli's a comin'
Better hide
Girl
Eli's a comin'
Better hide your heart
Your heart
Eli's comin'
Hide your heart
You better better hide your heart
Eli's comin' better walk
Cry but he's never gonna hear
Never gonna hear
And he ain't gonna follow
I cried
At the corners of the square
And everywhere I go
Eli's a comin'
Eli's a comin'
Eli's a comin' and he's comin'
To get me mama
I'm down on my knees
I'm down on my knees
Oh no no no
Hide it
Hide it
Hide it
Hide it
Hide it
Hide it
Hide it
Eli's comin' better hide your
    heart girl

50

Timer

Uptown
Goin' down
Ole life line
Walkin' down faster
Walkin' with the master of time
My lady woke up
And she broke down
She got up
She let go
Take me, Timer
Shake me, Timer
Timer, let it blow
Let it blow
My darling friends
Oh I belong to Timer
He changed my face
You're a fine one, Timer
You got me walkin'
Thru the gates of space
I keep rememberin'
Indoors
That I use to walk thru
Baby I'm not tryin' to talk you
    down
But I could walk thru them
    doors
Onto a pleasure ground
It was sweet and funny
A pleasure ground
Didn't know about money
Didn't know about Timer
Did not know about Timer
Holdin'
To my cradle
At the start

But now my hand is open
And now my hand is ready for
    my heart
So let the wind blow, Timer
Let the wind blow, Timer
I like her song
And if the song goes minor
I won't mind
And timer knows the lady's
    gonna
Love again
If you don't love me
The lady rambles
Never more
If you love me true
And if you love me true
I'll spend my life with you
And Timer
You're a jigsaw, Timer
You're a ...
God is a jigsaw
A jigsaw, Timer
You're a jigsaw, Timer
You're a ...
God is a jigsaw
A jigsaw, Timer
Timer
Soulin' with
Timer
Soulin' with
Timer
Soulin' with Timer
Let it blow

Tales of that album [*Eli and the Thirteenth Confession*] are legendary in the music business. Anyone who was paying attention and who was around at the time was just stunned by the depth of this record. She was like 20 at the time. It was a kind of music I hadn't heard before in terms of honesty and emotional depth. I heard the album before any of the covers came out. I listened to it end to end, and it was to me a whole cloth experience. It was not a bunch of songs. It was an opera in some ways.

—TODD RUNDGREN, ARTIST, FAN, AND PRODUCER

Stoned Soul Picnic

Surry down
To a stoned soul picnic
Surry down
To a stoned soul picnic
There'll be lots of time and wine
Red yellow honey
Sassafras and moonshine
Stoned soul

There'll be trains of blossoms
There'll be trains of music
There'll be trains of trust
Trains of golden dust
Come along surry
On sweet trains of thought

Can you surry?
Can you picnic?
Surry down
To a stoned soul picnic
Rain and sun come in akin
And from the sky
Come the Lord and the lightnin'
surry, surry, surry

Stoned Soul Picnic
(Picnic, A Green City)

Can you surry
Can you picnic?
Can you surry
Can you picnic?
Surry down
To a stoned soul picnic
Surry down
To a stoned soul picnic
There'll be lots of time and wine
Red yellow honey
Sassafras and moonshine
Red yellow honey sassafras
And moonshine
Stoned soul

Surry down
To a stoned soul picnic
Surry down
To a stoned soul picnic
Rain and sun come in akin
And from the sky come the Lord
And the lightnin'
And from the sky come the Lord
And the lightnin'
Stoned soul

Surry, surry, surry, surry
There'll be trains of blossoms
There'll be trains of music
There'll be trains of trust
Trains of golden dust
Come along and surry on
Sweet trains of thought
Surry on down

Can you surry?
Surry down
To a stoned soul picnic
Surry down
To a stoned soul picnic
There'll be lots of time and wine
Red yellow honey
Sassafras and moonshine
Red yellow honey sassafras
And moonshine moonshine
Stoned soul
Surry, surry, surry, surry
Surry, surry, surry
Surry, surry
Surry

One thing took place which I think is sad for all artists, especially artists like Laura Nyro. When Laura wrote the *Eli* record, there had been about three years between records, so she wrote the best songs she could possibly write while that window was open. Laura had the opportunity to be on her own for about three years and she wrote all these songs. When she wrote these songs she wasn't influenced by anybody. She sat in a little room and was virtually not successful. She had a couple of hit records but in her own mind the window of her ability was still open. After she finished the *Eli* record and people realized what was on that record, the next thing CBS said was, We want another record. They (CBS) have to take into consideration the kind of composer she was. She really wrote songs that were all babies, and she would put them in an incubator and she would nurse them to health.

—CHARLIE CALLELO, PRODUCER, *ELI AND THE THIRTEENTH CONFESSION*

Emmie
Oo la la la
Oo la la la la

Emily
And her love to be
Carved in a heart
On a berry tree
But it's only
A little farewell lovespell
Time to design a woman
Touch me
Oh wake me
Emily
You ornament the earth
For me

Oo la la la
Oo la la la la
Emily
You're the natural snow
The unstudied sea
You're a cameo
And I swear you were born—
A weaver's lover
Born for the loom's desire
Move me
Oh sway me
Emily
You ornament the earth
For me

You are my friend
And I love you
Emily

Emmie

Oo la la la

Emily
And her love to be
Carved in a heart
On a berry tree
But it's only a little farewell lovespell
Time to design a woman
Touch me
Oh wake me
Emily you ornament the earth
For me

Emily
You're the natural snow
The unstudied sea
You're a cameo
And I swear you were born
A weaver's lover
Born for the loom's desire
Move me
Oh sway me
Emily you ornament the earth for me

Emmie your mama's been a callin' you
Oo
Who stole
Mama's heart
And cuddled
In her garden? Darlin' Emmie
Oo la la la
You were my friend
And I loved you
Emily

The first Laura Nyro album I recall having a serious research project with, living with, and schlepping around with me everywhere was *Eli and the Thirteenth Confession*. That's the one I really got emotionally involved with.

—PHOEBE SNOW, ARTIST AND FAN

Woman's Blues

My lover's mouth
Been so good to me
My lover's mouth
Been so good to me
It promised joy for a jailhouse
And a broken key
Whoa God
I got a job
On the chamber's walls of
   heartache
Whoa God it's hard on the
   chamber's
Walls of heartache
Baby don't love me
Shuffle
'Cause another one do

My man's run off
Leave me motherless
My man's run off
Leave me motherless
That man
He ran just like a break in a dam
Whoa God
I got a job
On the chamber's walls of
   heartache
Whoa God it's hard on the
   chamber's walls of heartache
Baby don't love me
Shuffle
'Cause another one do
Another one too
Three four five seven
You'll never get to heaven

Don't talk wonder
'Cause God broke thunder above
You were lookin' to hurt
And I was hurtin' to love
My my well if it isn't everlovin'
   you

Go live as long as an elephant
Go live as long as an elephant
But there won't be
More lovin' woman than me
Whoa
Got to get gone better ride
From the hill on heartache
Whoa
Got to get gone better ride
From the hill on heartache
Baby don't love me
Shuffle 'cause another one
Baby don't love me?
Hitch hike

And damn be done

The rhythm effect that we created on "Eli's Comin'" I took from one of the records I made, which was "The Name Game," by Shirley Ellis. Basically, it was the trombones playing one and the upbeat of 3 and the other horns playing on one and two and the upbeat of three. All those musical things that were put into the mix created the element of "Eli." Laura felt that she would not be able to do the song justice if I did that. So she decided not to play on "Farmer Joe" and "Eli's Comin'."

—CHARLIE CALLELO, PRODUCER, *ELI AND THE THIRTEENTH CONFESSION*

Once It Was Alright Now (Farmer Joe)

Farmer Joe
I'm the meanest woman you know
She said farmer Joe
I'm the meanest ole woman you know
I let you slide about an hour ago

Farmer boy
Get your gun
Run run run–from love
Runnin' from the mindreader
Run baby run

Got a date
With the town shoe maker you know
She said I can't wait for your cornfields
Baby to grow
Whoa baby
Whoa baby
Get me my bags
And let the good wind blow
Get me my bags
And let the good wind blow
Get me my bags
And let the good wind blow
I've got to see about a man I know
Fire
Flames of gold rush my mind
Fire
Flames of gold rush my mind
Sock it to the railroad baby
Oo baby there's a train whistle comin'
Oo baby there's a train whistle comin'
Oo baby there's a train whistle comin'
Once it was alright now

When you spoke to her about music there would be a little gleam in her eye and she would go off into space. It's hard to explain, but whenever I would see Laura do this I knew that she was into a fantasy. There was sort of a childish glow about her as she tried to answer whatever question I presented to her. Like, Laura, how do you hear this? You could see the sparkle and she would go off into space and you would see her chuckle inside. She would not really know what she wanted it to sound like, although she would say she wanted it to be its own child or some statement that you would have to interpret to try to make some kind of musical sense. I said to her, "Let's go into the studio, just you and me, and let's record all these songs and put them all down with you singing." We went into the studio and in one day she recorded the entire *Eli* album on a piano, with Laura singing background vocals. I think if CBS were to look in the archive they would find that tape, which happens to be, in my opinion, something they should eventually release. None of anything that I was about to do appeared on those early recordings. It was just her voice and piano, and she did the background parts.

— CHARLIE CALLELO, PRODUCER, *ELI AND THE THIRTEENTH CONFESSION*

December Boudoir

Kisses from you
In the flames of December's
    boudoir
They fill me like melons
Touch me with chivalry
Truly I know, truly I know who
    you are
December will bear
Our affair
Running on streets of delight
And Decemberry ice
Oh see me I'm ageless
Loving you timelessly
Love colored soul, love colored
    soul
Kissing spice
Yes my love
I take my coffee in the mornin'
And all your love
A spoonful or so
Make us
Grow

Mama was clever
And my daddy loved her forever

Kisses from you
I'll remember
Kisses from you
In the flames of December
Kisses from you
True they are
Kisses from you in the flames
Of December's boudoir

Oo
Mainstream
Marzipan sweet
Bakin' out
In December heat

David [Geffen] set up a meeting and I went to her apartment one night. She had a one-bedroom apartment probably no bigger than maybe 15 by 20. Try to imagine this: myself, Laura, and David Geffen in a room with candles and Laura at this piano, which was slightly out of tune. Laura sat down and played the entire *Eli* album for me on the piano from beginning to end. She performed brilliantly. At the end of "The Confession" I was in tears.

—CHARLIE CALLELO, PRODUCER, *ELI AND THE THIRTEENTH CONFESSION*

The Confession

Super summer sugar coppin'
In the mornin'
Do your shoppin' baby
I love my love thing

You may leave the fair
But you'll be back I swear

Would you love to love me baby?
I would love to love you baby now
Would you love to love me baby?
I would love to love you baby now

Super summer sugar coppin'
In the mornin'
Do your shoppin' baby
I love my love thing

You may dissapear
But you'll be back I swear

Would you love to love me baby?
I would love to love you baby now
Would you love to love me baby?
I would love to love you baby
now

. I keep hearin' mother cryin' —
Thru the grave —
"Little girl, my daughter
You were born a woman
Not a slave"

Oh I hate my winsome lover
Tell him I've had others
At my breast
But tell him he had my heart
And only now am I a virgin
I confess

The Confession

Super summer sugar coppin'
In the morning
Do your shoppin' baby
Love my lovething
Super ride inside my lovething
You may disappear
But you'll be back I swear
Would you love
To love me baby
I would love
To love you baby now
Would you love
To love me baby
I would love
To love you baby now
Mama it's my pain
Super summer sugar coppin'
In the morning
Do your shoppin' baby
Love my lovething
Super ride inside my lovething
You may leave the fair
But you'll be back I swear
Would you love
To love me baby
I would love
To love you baby now
Would you love
To love me baby
I would love
To love you baby now
I keep hearin'
Mother cryin'
I keep hearin'
Daddy thru his grave

"Little girl
Of all the daughters
You were born a woman
Not a slave"
Oh I hate my winsome lover
Tell him I've had others
At my breast
But tell him he has held my
    heart
And only now am I a virgin
I confess

Love my lovething
Love is surely gospel

New York Tendaberry (1969)

The record that continues to move me the most, that I think is truly a masterpiece, is *New York Tendaberry*. On that album the song that moves me the most is "You Don't Love Me When I Cry," which opens the CD. To open a record with that song is incredibly courageous. It's groundbreaking, and the arrangement that was used on that song was groundbreaking, and the dynamic range of her vocal totally gives me goose bumps to this day.

—PETER GALLWAY, PRODUCER, *TIME AND LOVE: THE MUSIC OF LAURA NYRO*
(TRIBUTE ALBUM)

You Don't Love Me When I Cry

Two mainstream die
You don't love me when I cry
Have to say goodbye
I don't want to say goodbye
Baby goodbye

Mister I got funky blues
All over me
Such tender persuasion

I want to die
You don't love me when I cry
Made me love to play
Made me promise I would stay
Then you stayed away

Mister I got drawn blinds blues
All over me
Rubies and smoke rings
I will go

I will stay
In the hours of my crying day

"Captain for Dark Mornings" is my favorite Laura Nyro song. My mother's name was Lily and it was beautiful and haunting. I loved her straight-up pop stuff, too, but I liked it when she got a little left of center. That song was one of those things that played like a little mantra in your head.

—PHOEBE SNOW, ARTIST AND FRIEND

Captain for Dark Mornings

I am soft and silly
And my name is Lillianaloo
And sir
You're grace in action
To my satisfaction oo

Well my mama she's savin'
'Cause my daddy's a ravin'
Crazy gambler
But you
My captain
Are grace in action
To my satisfaction oo
Come along now

And I'll be your woman
If you'll be my captain
I'll be your woman
If you'll be my captain
I'll be your woman
If you'll be my fearless captain

Die I would lay me down and
   die
For my captain

I am soft and silly
And my name is Lillianaloo
And sir
You're fair black fashion
For this winter's passion oo

Well I been sold by sailors
I been worn by tailors
Soldiers wound me

But you
My captain
Are medication
For my reputation oo
Come along now

And I'll be your woman
If you'll be my captain
I'll be your woman
If you'll be my captain
I'll be your woman
If you'll be my fearless captain

Die I would lay me down and
   die
For my captain

Captain say yes

Tom Cat Goodbye

Rosie Pearl
Is a big blonde girl
And she sails around
Like a steamboat
Takes her time
And her eyes they shine
For Tom

Hey there, Tom Cat
Where've you been to?
Hey there, Tom Cat
Say where've you been to?
I'm so lonely
Been cryin'
Waitin' up for you
You hear that?
You hear that?
I got your name, Tom
I got your children
What about the children?
Tom Cat
Tom Cat
You ole rat
Where've you been to?

Johnny cheated
Frankie killed him
Johnny cheated
Say Frankie killed him
Shot and killed him
I don't blame her
I'd a done it too
You hear that?
You hear that?
You deal and promise

You kiss and swing lo
Footslippin' out the window
Tom Cat
Tom Cat
You ole rat
Where've you been to?...

Mercy on Broadway

Madison smiled
And she hung with a band of
   strays
The band was gone
Bringin' it on
To the Broadway blaze
Once I lived under the city in my
   sweet July

July mercy on Broadway
Don't you believe it
You better know what I say
She'll make you pay
Down the alleyway
Slippin' up a sidestreet
Shine
Everybody
Shine

On Broadway
Jive and pray
There ain't no mercy now
On Broadway

People and the landlords shine
Down and gay wine
In the doom swept the band
   away
Baby on Broadway
Is she mild
Like mother and child?
Does she obey?
Once I lived under the city in my
   sweet July

July mercy on Broadway
Don't you believe it
You better know what I say
She'll make you pay
Black city fair
Ole road runner there
Shine
Everybody
Shine

Looking back to the mid-'60s, when Bob Dylan started to blow up, she was starting to come out with her stuff. That was the soundtrack to a lot of people's lives. People were deciding whether or not they were going to do this. If you listen to her, and you listen to everybody else that is out now, how could she not have been influential to almost anybody?

—**PHOEBE SNOW,** ARTIST AND FAN

Save the County

Come on people
Come on children
Come on down to the glory river
Gonna wash you up
And wash you down
Gonna lay the devil down
Come on people
Come on children
There's a king at the glory river
And the precious king
He loved the people to sing
Babes in the blinkin' sun
Sang we shall overcome!
Come on people, sons and mothers
Keep the dream
Of the two young brothers
Gonna take the dream
And ride the dove
We could build the dream with love

I got fury in my soul
Fury's gonna take me to the glory goal
In my mind I can't study war no more
Save the people
Save the children
Save the country

Gibsom Street

Don't go to Gibsom cross the river
The devil is hungry
The devil is sweet
If you are soft then you will shiver
They hang the alley cats on Gibsom street

I wish my baby were forbidden
I wish my world
Be struck by sleet
I wish to keep my mirror hidden
To hide the eyes that looked on Gibsom street

There is a man he knows where I'm going
Gave me a strawberry
To eat
I sucked its juices never knowing
That I would sleep that night on Gibsom street

A great thing, when we used to be on the bus, was she would always say, "Do you think we could live here?" This is how family oriented she was about the band. It didn't matter—whatever town we were in, it was almost as if she would love it if the whole band just lived in a house and we were a family.

—JIMMY VIVINO, GUITARIST AND LAURA NYRO BANDLEADER

Time and Love

So winter froze the river
And winter birds don't sing
So winter makes you shiver
So time is gonna bring you
   spring

So he swears he'll never marry
Says that cuddles are a curse
Just tell him plain
You're on the next train
If love don't get there first

Time and love
Everybody
Time and love
Nothing cures like
Time and love
Don't let the devil fool you
Here comes a dove
Nothing cures like Time and love

So winter froze the river
And winter birds don't sing
So winter makes you shiver
So time is gonna bring you
   spring

You been runnin', you been
   ramblin'
And you don't know what to do
A holy golden wager says
That love will see you through

Time and love

So Jesus was an angel
And mankind broke his wing
But Jesus gave his lifeline
So sacred bells could sing

Now a woman is a fighter
Gathered white or african
A woman
Is a woman inside
Has miracles for her man

Time and love

Man Who Sends Me Home

There's a man who loves me
When it hurts inside
There's a man who loves me
When my hair is tied
When my hair is down
When I touch the man
Lord I rise
To rooftops in his eyes

Never never
Never will I roam
'Cause he's the man
Who sends me home.

Sweet Lovin' Baby

I belong
To the man
Don't belong without him
When I sleep without him
Loneliness
Loneliness
My dreams with God
Softly waiting
I belong to the man

Sweet lovin' baby
Oh sweet lovin' baby
I want you
I could almost die
He says
There's gold in you darling
Drew gold
When I woke her
She's an ole chain smoker
Grace
And the Preacher
Blown fleets of sweet eyed
   dreams
Tonight
Loneliness
Loneliness
Natural windmill
Wheel weave and bless
My bed
My bed
My man

That's lovin' baby
Oh sweet lovin' baby
Where is the night luster?

Past my trials
Sparkling in flight
In your arms
For all of my life

Captain Saint Lucifer

Mama, mama
You're a whiz and a scholar too
Mama open up the room lock
Sip, sip
I'm going to the moon dock
He gives to me

Buckles off shingles
Off a cockleshell on Norway
   basin
Coke and tuna
Boots and roses from Russia

Now I'll live and die and rise
With my captain
Mama say go

Meet me Captain Saint Lucifer
Darling I'll be there
Don't you know
Meet me Captain Saint Lucifer
Darling I'll be there
Don't you know
Now don't you know I love you?

Meet me Captain Saint Lucifer
La la la la la la la la
Oo I love you
Love you I do

Mama, mama
You're a whiz and a scholar too
Mama I'm at anchor in your
   glow now
Sip, sip

Even as I go now
He gives to me

Buckles off shingles
And a jangle from a congo love
   chase
Early bloomers
Made of earth and love lace

Now I'll live and die and rise
With my captain
Mama be happy

Meet me Captain Saint Lucifer
Darling I'll be there
Don't you know
Meet me Captain Saint Lucifer
Darling I'll be there
Don't you know

Gutters in stacks
Is where I come from
Buckles off a poverty drum
Oh my love trumpet soul
Tell Gabriel
To tell the captain

Thank you baby
You're my baby now

She loved them [her songs]. How could she not? She wrote some lovely lines, some magical thoughts, and she had the gift, that little gift.

— ROSCOE HARRING, LAURA'S SOUND ENGINEER, ROAD MANAGER

New York Tendaberry

New York Tendaberry
Blueberry
A rush on rum
Of brush and drum
And the past is a blue note
Inside me
I ran away in the morning

New York Tendaberry
Blueberry
Rugs and drapes and drugs
And capes
Sweet kids in hunger slums
Firecrackers break
And they cross
And they dust
And they skate
And the night comes

I ran away in the morning

Now I'm back
Unpacked
Sidewalk
And pigeon
You look like a city
But you feel like a religion
To me

New York Tendaberry
True berry

I lost my eyes
In east wind skies
Here where I've cried

Where I've tried
Where God and the tendaberry
  rise
Where quakers and
  revolutionaries
Join for life
For precious years
Join for life
Through silver tears

New York Tendaberry

Christmas And The Beads of Sweat (1970)

Brown Earth

Morning
Came to the windows
Of the street
Sellin' red watermelon
Five cents a piece
Merry boat on the river
Freedom
Fresh dreams to deliver
Freedom
Over and over and over
I call out your name

God standing on the brown
    earth
"Get up" mama hollers
Shooflies in my doorway
White dove's gonna come today
White dove's gonna come today
Oh what a morning
I feel so good
Oh what a morning
Of brotherhood

Hold me by the light
Kittens run the neighborhood
    through
Ragamuffin boys
All the world is new
By the light of day

Give with your heart
And love will come to you
Kids come in all shapes and
    colors
To the cool morning dew

Merry boat on the river
Freedom
Fresh dreams to deliver
Freedom
Over and over and over
And over and over and over

God standing on the brown
    earth
Lovelight in the morning
Shooflies in my doorway
White doves gonna come today!

When I was a kid my mission in life was to meet Laura, to play music with her, and to be her friend. I had no agenda as to how all this was going to happen. But I was clear. I started writing notes to Laura and sending her flowers upstairs. She had my phone number. One day she called me on a Saturday afternoon and asked me if I was busy. She asked me if I had ever seen the movie *Black Orpheus*. I was flabbergasted; you can imagine. She loved that movie. I told her I had never seen it. I said, "Yeah, I think I can do that." I went to Laura's house and it's just she and I. We're sitting around eating tuna fish on Saltine crackers when the phone rang. It was Vicky Wickham, manager of LaBelle, and Laura was telling me she was going to be doing an oldies album to pay homage to her roots. That was the music that she grew up listening to. Patty LaBelle and the Bluebells were one of her favorite vocal groups at the time. She was telling me how she was trying to meet them so they could possibly do this record *Gonna Take a Miracle* together. Vicky said to Laura, "Patty and the girls are available this afternoon and would love to get together with you." Would it be okay to come over? Of course Laura was thrilled. Now she felt [about them] like I felt about her. Laura gets off the phone and says, "Nydia, would you mind if we didn't go to the movies? Vicky is bringing Patty LaBelle and Sarah Dash and Nona Hendrix over." I said, "No, I don't think I would mind." This is when "Lady Marmalade" was at its peak. LaBelle was very big at that point. They talked a little bit, she told them her idea about doing *Gonna Take a Miracle*, and Laura sat down at the piano and started playing "Nowhere to Run," "Jimmy Mack." She played a bunch of oldies. The girls started to sing with her. What we did on the record is pretty much how they sang it right from the get-go.

—NYDIA "LIBERTY" MATA, PERCUSSIONIST WITH LAURA AND WITH HARPBEAT

When I Was a Freeport and You Were the Main Drag

You took my heart misery
You taught me blues
Well I got a lot of patience baby
That's a lot of patience to lose
I'm crying
I'm mad at my country
Now I've been treated bad
When I was a freeport and you were the main drag

Broken blues
I just don't know
Little bird, flying by my window
Take me when you go
I'm crying
I'm looking at these times
And it's bound to drive me mad
When I was a freeport and you were the main drag

What did I do?
Everybody's putting me down
I keep runnin'
But the law kept comin' around

So faretheewell happiness
'Cause I got the blues
And I got a lot of patience baby
That's a lot of patience to lose
I'm a woman
Waiting for due time
Now I've been treated bad
When I was a freeport and you were the main drag

Blackpatch

Invitations to my party
Send Jones an inviting card
He got his meanstreak from the gutter
Got his kindness from God

Now tugboats paint the river
Carry coal to the city
And white dock liners
Happiness on the uptown side
At my party in the morningtide
Oh la la la blackpatch

Clothespins on wash ropes
Window to window tie
Socks and bells and nightgowns
Tassels in the morning sky

Womanchild on the sidestreet
Flashin' in blackpatch
Lipstick on her reefer
Waiting for her match...

Been on a Train

Been on a train
Baby did you hear the whistle
  blow?
Been on a train north
Baby did you hear the whistle
  blow?
I saw a man take a needlefull of
  hard drug
And die slow

Been on a train
And I'm never gonna be the
  same

There's a bright light in the
  north wind
Gonna bring you home
Mister there's a bright light in
  the north wind
It's gonna bring you home
He said "Sweet darling woman
Leave me alone"

Been on a train
And I'm never gonna be the
  same

You got more tracks on you baby
Then the tracks of this train
You got no guts, no gospel
And you got no brain
He said "I got just one thing
Gonna soothe my pain"
No, no
Damn you mister

And I dragged him out the door
Damn you mister
And I dragged him out the door
He died in the morning sun
And I won't go north no more

I suspect there's a train
Going north in a month or two
I still hear his words
He said "There's nothing left to
  say or do"
But mister you were wrong
And I'm gonna sing my song for
  you

Been on a train
And I'm never gonna be the
  same

Upstairs by a Chinese Lamp

Market in the cool white morning
Merchants sell as ladies buy
Milk, tobacco, soap and matches
Sweep the floor while dishes dry

Spring whispered in her ear
Like soft mediterranean wailin'

Sleepy woman by the window
Dreaming in the morning air
Of the man who takes her sweetness
By a Chinese lamp upstairs

The steam of china tea
You could hear the woman sing
In the soft flames of spring

Spring has swept the scarlet sidestreets
Winds caress, undress, invite
Upstairs by a Chinese lamp
They softly talk in the cool spring night

Laura gave me a harp in 1976. She had been doing her *Seasons of Light* tour, and Nydia and I, who had grown up together, met her basically at the same time. I met Laura through Nydia's persistence as a die-hard fan. She got through the wall and, once Laura got to know Nydia, she fell in love with her, and then she fell in love with me. We were all very close from that point on. The year she gave me the harp I think was the second tour we had gone on with her. I used to travel with her also, but more or less as a mascot. I didn't do much, but we used to travel together. I was about 24 at the time. I hadn't yet found my calling. I was looking for something. Laura had bought this harp a couple of years before when she was hanging out with Alice Coltrane. Alice played the harp and she encouraged Laura to get one, which she did. They were doing these Swami Sachidinanda retreats where they would hang out a lot together.

The harp is a very demanding instrument. It's not the type of instrument you can play around with. You have to get into it or forget it. Laura loved the harp, but never pursued it that much, although she had taken some lessons. She had to cut her nails, and she didn't like to cut her nails. You cannot play the classical harp with nails.

She had this harp in the house and I saw it from time to time when I went up to her place. She lived in the Beresford, right near the planetarium. She was in the penthouse and had a beautiful view of the park. I would see this harp up there, and I was enchanted by it but it was like a Martian to me, it was such a foreign thing. It was beautiful and very foreign. All during the *Seasons of Light* tour we would talk about *what is Ellen going to do with her life*. We would get into philosophical conversations. I think it came up a couple of times that I liked the harp, or maybe I told Nydia I liked the harp. On Channel 13 I had seen a woman play jazz on the harp with a bass and all the jazz instruments. When I saw that, I said to myself if I had a harp I could do it. I had a feeling that I could play.

When we came back from the tour, Laura was going to be giving up her place at the Beresford and moving lock, stock, and barrel to her land in Danbury. She had bought that land from Swami Sachidinanda. It's beautiful land with stones and trees lending themselves to meditation. She bought this land and was living in the city. I guess she realized that she needed to be in one place, and she decided to give up the Beresford. A couple of days after we came back from the tour Laura called me up and, in her casual way, she said "I'm moving and I'm trying to prune down. Would you like me to send the harp over?" I was flabbergasted! I said yeah, sounds like a great possibility for me. She said there is no pressure. She wasn't expecting me to become a master. She said just take it and see what you think. I was so ready to bite off something, and I was lucky enough.

—ELLEN URYEVICK, FRIEND, HARPIST IN HARPBEAT

Map to the Treasure

Where is your woman?
Gone to Spanish Harlem
Gone to buy you pastels

Where is your woman?
Gone to Spanish Harlem
Gone to buy you books and bells
Beneath indian summer

Take my hand now
There is a land now
In the treasure of love

Jade and coral
Perfume from Siam
In the treasure of love

To your fingertips
To the summer sunset
In the treasure of love
In the treasure of love
In the treasure of love
Light the night
Oh light the night
Come my way
Light the night

Come to me baby
You got the look that I adore
That I understand
My pretty medicine man
My
Pretty
Medicine man
Got pretty medicine in his hand

For you I bear down
Soft and burning
In the treasure of love
In the treasure of love
In the treasure of love
Love

Where is your woman?
Gone to Spanish Harlem
Gone to buy you pastels

Beads of Sweat

Cold jade wind
Not an angel in the sky
Just cold jade restless wind
Somethin's comin' I know
To devastate
My soul

I pricked my fingers
On the thorns
And this rain is a-rainin' hard
This sky's gonna beckon Mariah
To match my soul
Rain in the river
Rain in the river
Rain on the river banks
Down my neck
Beads of sweat

Rain on the highway
Running clear across New York
A windsong through the barren
    trees
Wild lavender heather
By the railroad sways
Listen to the wailin'
Of the rain in the river
Rain on the river banks
Roll, roll
River rock his soul
She's calling you
Rainclouds
Rainclouds
Roll, roll
River rock his soul
She's calling you

Rainclouds
Rainclouds
Down his neck
Down his neck
Down his neck
Beads of
Beads of
Beads of
Beads of sweat

Five boys standing
On the banks of the river
Waiting for the virgin snow
Searching for a miracle
A pearl in an oyster
And we all looked out to God
Although he is the color of the
    wind
Listen to the wailing
Of the rain in the river
Rain on the river banks

Come young braves
Come young children
Come to the book of love with
    me
Respect your brothers and your
    sisters
Come to the book of love
I know it ain't easy
But we're gonna look for a better
    day
Come young braves
Come young children

I had never met anybody with perfect pitch. Someone who could tell you what note you were singing was pretty amazing. She had perfect pitch.

—ROSCOE HARRING, LAURA'S SOUND ENGINEER, ROAD MANAGER

Christmas in My Soul

I love my country
As it dies
In war and pain
Before my eyes
I walk the streets
Where disrespect has been
The sins of politics
The politics of sin
The heartlessness that darkens
    my soul
On Christmas

Red and silver
On the leaves
Fallen white snow
Runs softly through the trees
Madonnas weep
For the wars of hell
They blow out the candles
And haunt Noel
The missing love that rings
    through the world
On Christmas

Black panther brothers
Bound in jail
Chicago seven
And the justice scale
Homeless indian
Of Manhattan isle
All god's sons have gone to trial
And all god's love is out of style
On Christmas

Now the time has come to fight

Laws in the book of love burn
    bright
People you must win
For thee America
Her dignity
For all the high court world to
    see
On Christmas

Christmas in my soul

Christmas in my soul

Christmas in my soul

Joy to the world

Smile (1976)

Children of the Junks

Children of the Junks
Slant-eyed
Children of the Junks
Go by
Mama's comin' soon
And the junks are turning in the
Spring sky

Dragon rings
Tax-free things
Forever
People pick and pay
'Til the day fades away
Cooling in the wind
"Comrades all"
Red papers ring

Flowers in the sun
Shining
On the children of the world
Night comes
Sleep for me
Ain't nothin' just a moonstruck junk
On the sea
Kowloon

All the junks are sleeping
Spinning flowers on the shade
All the junks are sleeping
But alley cats and renegades

Money

She said
"I'm young enough
I'm old enough
To paint a smile
I tasted heaven and hell
Heaven stay a while"

A good friend
Is a rare find
Their straight talk
Can ease your mind
A good pimp's
Gonna rob you blind

Money, money, money
I feel like a pawn
In my own world
I found the system
and I lost the pearl

It's breaking me down
Well you wake
You don't shake
You just make the sound
Go round and round and round
And round

Bleed a little
Bleed a little
Till your freedom calls you

Somewhere out
Children laugh
Like meteors
Rolling down the grass

Mother's pull the nighttime in
Calling for their children
With spoons in the wind
But not for me

She said
"I'm young enough
I'm old enough
In the city machine
Where industries
Fill the fish
Full of mercury
(It's tax free)"
She said
"My struggle hurt
But it turned me on
And when my revolution came
The chain was gone
On my feet
To the sound of my heartbeat"

Money, money, money
Do you feel like a pawn
In your own world?
You found the system
And you lost the pearl

Like leaves coming down
You've got to wake, shake
Make your vibe go 'round
And round and round and round

I'm going to paraphrase a story that I think is quintessential Laura. Have you come across Roscoe Harring? He was an early member of the 5th Avenue Band. He went on to be a road manager for John Sebastian, Laura's road manager and Laura's manager. He was even a co-producer on the *Smile* record. Roscoe told a story at the service for Laura after her death. This is quintessential Laura. Laura played Wolman Skating Rink in Central Park at what was called the Schaeffer Music Festival. She showed up for sound check in the middle of the afternoon. The show was to start at 7:00. She goes up on the stage and goes "Oh my goodness, this is way too high. Roscoe, can you have them lower the stage? It's just too far from the people." Roscoe looks at Laura and in a gentle, managerial way says, "Laura, this festival is running all summer. It's taken weeks to create all this. I just don't think there is any way they can lower the stage." She takes a beat or two and she looks at Roscoe and she says, "Well, can we bring the people up?" That is Laura all the way.

— PETER GALLWAY, PRODUCER, *TIME AND LOVE: THE MUSIC OF LAURA NYRO*
(TRIBUTE ALBUM)

I Am the Blues

Cigarettes
I'm all alone with my smoke and
   ashes
Cigarettes
I'm all alone with my smoke and
   ashes
Take me night-flying
Maybe Mars has good news
Who? Who am I?
I am the blues

Soothe me
Horn's warm red love makin'
Funky music
Move me
Night wind, red tail lights and
Funky music
'Cause I'm restless
In my love for sale shoes
Who? Who am I?
I am the blues

In a world of war
I can't find my laughter
I can't see the night sun
And I can't see my freedom
I guess I can't see too much no
   more
Baby 'til I lose my blues
Fly thru the sky like superfly
Over the stars we climb
Over this sweet red wine
I tell myself
Right on
Right on

Right on
Right on
Blues
Flying so high
A plane in the sky
Listen to the music of the night
   wind

Stormy Love

You were my darlin' light
Everything was gonna be alright

And you were my everything
Boy once you could make me sing

Well I ain't gonna fly away
And I ain't gonna cry all day

But I might spread my wings
I've gotta do so many things

And I'm gonna love again
Though I'm never gonna be the same
And baby it's the last dance
I just can't believe it
Baby it's the last dance
My mind won't let me sleep
And baby it's a stormy love

And this world may knock my looks
And this world may burn my books
But I ain't gonna fly away
I ain't gonna cry all day
But I might spread my wings
I've gotta do so many things
And I'll turn my red light on
Let it shine when the sun is gone
And baby it's the last dance
Soon I will be leaving
Baby it's the last dance
I'll pack my boots and pearls
Baby, it's a stormy world

And you were my everything

Cat Song

My name is Eddie
I am a cat
And I sleep with one eye open
Watching the morning sail

Someone calls "Eddie"
Up to their lap
And I purr
But I'd sure like to get me
My breakfast
Especially a fishtail
Turn it into a fishscale

No I'm not
Like you people
You wheel and you war
And you white wash your day away
(Where you goin')
On my merry way

Spring full of fire
Up goes a flower-kite
Run now
Sleep in the sun now
I like my fun now

My name is Eddie
I am a cat
And I sleep with one eye open
Meow

Laura was very unusual. She was like a flower that needed to be taken care of delicately. She was into her own space. She was extremely sensitive about things. Not emotionally sensitive, but she paid attention to details. We were working on a song and I asked her what she wanted the song to sound like. She stared out into space and a little childish giggle came on her face and she looked at her chair. She said, "Charlie, I want it to be like my chair." I looked at the chair. The chair was very plain, it was all wood. You could see the wood grain in it. What she really was trying to explain to me was that she wanted the song to be really organic in nature. That it would have acoustic instruments. That it would not be brassy. It would be delicate and cared for and curved in the right places. It was a song on the *Smile* record. I don't remember which song it was. When we went to the studio and she listened back to it I said, "Laura does this sound like your chair." She giggled and said "Yes, Charlie, it sounds like my chair." The last time I saw her was in the late '80s when she was performing in California. I saw her performing onstage and she was having such a great time. To see the fans and to listen to the way she developed the songs she was performing and how the fans reacted to them was thrilling to see.

—CHARLIE CALLELO, PRODUCER, *ELI AND THE THIRTEENTH CONFESSION*

Midnite Blue

Midnite blue
You make me laugh
You make me tremble
But I'm as strong as you
Midnite blue
Midnite blue
You're funny
And I like you too
Shy, sly, gypsy high now
You could buck the sky now
Midnite blue

There's smoke in the kitchen
Shrimps curled
The sun on black velvet
And high stars
At the bottom of the world
Smile all you want
But you know
That I'm fine
In the warm hands
Of midnite blue

Now the river music haunts me
It's spirit calling me
Where's my midnite blue?
I need his melody
Oh midnite blue
Come to me
Oh midnite blue
I need your melody
I need your melody
I need the rhythm of your melody
'Cause I love you
Midnite blue

Smile

Winter
Turn on the night
Turn on your love-light
I'm a non-believer
But I believe
In your smile
Well I wanna talk to you baby
On brandy-wine
Mars in the stars
Mars is a-risin'
Mars in the stars
Mars is a-risin'
And I feel like I'm way
In deep dream baby
Feel like I'm way in a deep dream
Yes

Lovers
Light in the inn
What are they thinking?
Patterns falling
Down the sky
And the fire
And the kiss
Of the cunt-tree night
Your tender strong freaky love
Strangers and mountains
Are blurred in a snowflight
Mars in the stars
Mars is a-risin'
Mars in the stars
Mars is a-risin'
The world's insane
The paper's gone mad
But our love is a peace vibe
Yes

Season Of Lights ...
Laura Nyro In Concert (1977)

Morning News

The morning news is wet from the rain
Letters are blurred down the page
Morning news filled my head, it said business is fine
War and business make the man
He stole the sky in the indian land
His wife helped him for the free, cooking and cleaning
Silently
Mountains so high
Freedom sang how you shall end to the critical life
Of the corporate design
Mountains so high, page three is crazy
With your authorities
Near or far
Love is on

Two worlds spin in time
One around you and one inside
And the morning news is wet from the rain
Letters are blurred down the page
The TV set may numb your brain

Nested (1978)

Will Lee has a great story where they were recording *Nested* or *Mother's Spiritual* and Laura stopped the take and said, "Will, can we work on the bass sound? Can you make the bass sound more like this wicker chair?" She always spoke in colors with music—more red, more green, more blue.

—JIMMY VIVINO, GUITARIST AND LAURA NYRO BANDLEADER

Mr. Blue
(The Song of Communications)

"Hello"
He said, "Hello?"
"I'd like to see you"
He said, "Look sweetheart
You know what happens
When we get together
I mean I've heard of liberation
But sweetheart
You're in outer space"

Oh Mr. Blue
I've been studying the radar in
   the sky
I can almost run, fly
Listen like the animals do
I'm ready to meet the crew
Yes I'm ready for you

Earth calling you
I've been a gypsy fire
Warm desire
You've seen this too
Roger and out Mr. Blue

This is the song of
   communications
Sending out peace vibrations
Genuine cause
To end our wars
Or is this the song of
   complications?
A hopeless declaration?
Can we mend
Transcend

The broken dishes of our love?
Our conflicts?
Can we be friends?

"Hello"
He said, "Hello?"
"This is your copilot"
He said, "Yeah
Look sweetheart
I've loved you – but
You can be so arrogant
And you don't know anything
About being cool"

Oh Mr. Blue
I've been studying the radar in
   the sky
Measuring earth and time
The rainbows on your pillow are
   new
I'm a fucking mad scientist too
Baby let the one who loves you
   come thru
Baby come thru
Earth calling
You
Come thru
Calling calling
Mr. Blue

Italics indicates spoken lyrics.

She was one of the better writers of our era and we had some good ones. She was writing in the big bull ring, if you will. That is, she had hits at the time when the likes of the Beatles and Beach Boys and the big boys were shooting at the charts. So the competition was stiff—not for the fainthearted; and she was right there. I also wasn't faint of heart when it came to being a fan of hers. I let her know that if she was going to have a harmonica, I bloody wanted to be the harmonica player.

—JOHN SEBASTIAN, ARTIST AND FRIEND

Rhythm & Blues

Mama where's my silver shoes?
Mama where is my perfume?
Mama said, "Don't go down"
But tonite my baby's
Gonna take me downtown

Rock me, roll me, rhythm and
   blues
Rock me, roll me, rhythm and
   blues
Daddy said, "Don't go down"
But tonite the blue fox
Is gonna take me downtown

(Blue fox brought me flowers)
He said
"We'll harmonize by starlight
Party-light
Currents of music
Thru the fields
And country nights
Music
Be good to yourself
It's the least you can do
Be good to yourself
It's the most you can do"
Mr. Fox, I'm ready
Baby, baby, baby
I'm feelin' half crazy
My heart is burnin'
Burnin' for rhythm and blues

Rock me, roll me, rhythm and
   blues

Rock me, roll me, rhythm and
   blues
Mama said, "Don't go down"
But tonite my baby's gonna
Take me downtown

Italics indicates spoken lyrics.

She wanted to show me some ideas she had, so she handed me some notes on a paper plate that started from the center of the plate; she wrote circular, outwards in a spiral, towards the edges. So you start in the middle of the plate and find yourself turning this plate as you're reading her notes. They were just thoughts about the music, about songs, about what we were going to do. I thought that was inspired.

—JIMMY VIVINO, GUITARIST AND LAURA NYRO BANDLEADER

Emmie
Oo la la l.

And when I die

My Innocence/Sophia

Innocence
My innocence
Comes from my mother

Innocence
My innocence
Comes from my warm
Earth mother

Oh – have you heard
I wanna celebrate the word

My innocence
My innocence
I gave to my lover
To his lips

Innocence
My innocence

Oh – have you heard
I'm gonna celebrate the word

Hecate
Queen of the nite
Queen of the bold
Shine your lite
Down the open road

Midnite in my eyes
Highway in my hair
I don't want no diamond rings
I got all my pretty things

Sophia
Goddess of wisdom serene
Shine your lite
Shine your lite
For a gypsy queen
In a midnite dream

Innocence
My innocence
Is a wild thing

Innocence
My innocence

Unknown future
It's me and you now
Unknown moon
Floating past her
Mother earth are you hiding
In the laughter
Of my innocence?

My Innocence

My innocence, my innocence
Comes from my mother
My innocence, my innocence
Comes from my warm earth mother
Out along the gravestones
The sky is speechless
And my mind
It blows away

My innocence, my innocence
I gave to my lover
To his lips
My innocence, my innocence
I gave to my cold, cold lover
Earth under my feet
Splits in the sun
The nest blows away
The sweet summer days die young

I look for the man
With the Indian hair
I look for his land
But it isn't there
In our room tonight
Sharing the moon
To fight the pain

My innocence, my innocence
Is a wild thing
My innocence, my innocence
Unknown future it's me and you now
Unknown moon floating past her
Mother earth are you hiding in the laughter
Of my innocence?

Child of the Universe

Bb - A D F (F?)
2:50 end   ys be
Taking it out - 4+   a lot
                     is not

Broke...   e World

Oh star
Shine on me
I'm ju... again in the universe   maaa zine ?
I con...
and...
in the...
Could...
to a...

Oh :
There...
of...
And...
und...
Ro...
An...

1978 ✓

Crazy love

Key - G   80F
4:00 with nice
touch down +
00's like "fly and
away", message
to micheal
To light the
way rythmn.

Oh gypsy man
The river has seen
our lost melodies
with their notes so warm
moon banjo
down a river in the breeze
He was singin catfish blues
split apart
shot thru the heart
why did you make me feel
this need
Crazy love
My name is in your blood
+ what (this)(your) true love's
done to me
___

You blew thru my life
Some fleeting years ago
from the midwest plains
and rivers
to find the peace to grow
I ~~be~~was burnin
and you walked soft
~~talked soft~~
like an animal
on silent feet
on a block of snow
You were looking for a true love
to light the way

But it's all gone
with your deer's eyes
and your ways of steel
You could travel miles + miles
in a blind ree
but I'd know you crazy love
And turn (my) foolish heart away.

Oh my lover
father of my unborn star
I may ache behind your snake cold
but my will is as strong   back
with your deer's eyes I know so well
your ways of steel   as you are
I wonder if I ever knew you?   your
Crazy love - it's a crazy love   your
I'm empty from your weakness
Pregnant with the knowledge
the flame of ~~your~~ true love

Crazy Love

Gypsy man
The river has seen
Our lost melodies
With their notes so warm
Moon banjo
Down a river in the breeze
He was singing
Catfish blues
Split apart
Shot thru the heart
Why did you make me feel this
   need
Crazy love, my name is in your
   blood
And what your true love's done
   to me

You blew through my life
Some fleeting years ago
From the midwest plains and
   rivers
To find the peace to grow
I was burning
And you walked soft
Talked soft
Like an animal
On silent feet
On a block of snow
You were looking for a true love
To light the way

But it's all gone
With your deer's eyes
And your ways of steel
You could travel miles and miles

In a blind reel
But I'd know you crazy love
And turn my foolish heart away

Oh my lover
Father of my unborn star
I may ache behind your snake
   cold back
But my will is as strong as you
   are
With your deer's eyes
I know so well
Your ways of steel
I wonder if I ever knew you?
Crazy love, it's a crazy love
I'm empty from your weakness
Pregnant with the knowledge
And the flame of your true love

American Dreamer

Autumn's child is catchin' hell
For having been too naive to tell
Property rights from chapel bells
"There's nothing we can do
We could not get there in time
It's too late
She signed on the dotted line"

Oh shoot 'em up
Cops and robbers
Oh America

The manager smiled
He said, "We're gonna straighten
  this mess"
He had a picture of Spot
And Jane on his desk
So I signed his strange contract
With the transparent lines
"There's nothing we can do
We could not get there in time
It's too late
She signed on the dotted line"

Oh shoot 'em up
Cops and robbers
Oh America

The lawyers cried
Thru the telephone rings
The doctors sighed
"She's imagining things"
When he came thru the window
With those crazy eyes
Dick Tracy in disguise

He said, "You need a guiding
  hand
You're soft and you're fine
Sign here on the dotted line"

Oh big deals
Cops and robbers
Oh America
I am your rose
American dreamer
Flyin' high
And down thru America
Didn't you know
American dreamer
Flyin' high
And down thru America
America
America

Springblown

I've been waiting
A clock on the wall
Still
Every time that I see your face
It's like a warm embrace
That's all

And I've been waiting baby
To set my soul free
Still baby
Every time that I see your face
It's like a warm embrace
To me

Maybe it's the spring night blowing
Thru the pines and the amber gem
All my life I'm searching
For celestial harmony
Pretty baby love me again
And again and again

I worry
Worry maybe
I'm calling your name
You know
Seeds of our baby

Spring song
Am I weak or strong?
A rose is pressing
Thru a clock on the wall
I can't wait too long
Every time that I see your face
It's like a warm embrace to me
Everytime...anytime

Sweet Sky

Stand up straight
Watch your time
Learn the rules
Be cool
Stay in line
Oh but
I'm still mixed up
Like a teenager
Gone like the 4th of July
For the sweet sky

What do I care anymore
These rules make me bored
The same old rap
The same old gap
It had me once before
But that's when I was
Mixed up like a teenager
Now I'm gone like the 4th of
   July
For the sweet sky
The sweet sky

I'm free if I can be me
You're free if you just be
I'm free if I can be me
Naturally, naturally, naturally

Oh my sweet love
I'm open to you
To laugh with you
Talk to you
Reel some rhythm and blues
I'll rock you all night
Don't put off this fire

I'm burnin' like the 4th of July
Or should I be shy for the sweet
   sky?
'Cause my love is high

People are beautiful
As they pass by
This rhythm is beautiful

Light-Pop's Principle

You are light
The same energy
That makes the sun shine bright!
You are light
You're the energy
Atoms and light

Sage's light
Oh and Edison
He made two sparks ignite
All you do
It's a scientific chain reaction
It'll come back to you
You better do it right

In your flight
Send your love out
To the planet's soul
'Cause all are one
And all the living things they need
Some light to grow

Laura liked simple things. One of her favorite things was to have a big pajama party. Her thing was that we'd all go to her house or my mom's apartment. We'd all sleep on the floor and have rice and beans, and she would be thrilled with that. It would be Laura, Maria, Gil, me, my mother, maybe a couple of dogs. Six of us in a small room and we would watch movies. She was a kid at heart. She had the best giggle of anybody I know.

—NYDIA "LIBERTY" MATA, PERCUSSIONIST WITH LAURA AND WITH HARPBEAT

1978

Crazy love

Key - G ᴮᴰᶠ
4:00 with nice
touch down +
00's like "fly
away", message.

Rainbow 4:30
(song of the homeless)
G - BDF
3:00, new end - 2:00

Oh gypsy m...
The river ha...
our l...
with
moon
down
He wa...
split...
shot...
Why...
this...
Craz...
my r...
+ wh...
done...

To a child
(Bill's song)

Wo...
This is a song
from the K...
The moonli...
"Hey mother...
Is there m...
(An ra...
Talk to me...
"Well you...
brand new...
We are fi...
We're wri...
a note to...
Send it...
to Nicar...
Then do...
(don't l...
lost in...
Oh (send...

And this...
from the...
"We love...
(Sweet a...
(speed f...

"But Co...
C...

New m...
We bon...
To live...
freedom...
to to w...
(Sleepy,...
starr...
Good...
If Ni...
a' all...
a' (sent)...

You...
Som...
from...
and...
to f...
I b...
and...
talk...
like...
on s...
On a...
You...
to k...
But...
wit...
and...
You...
In...
but...
And...

Oh n...
fath...
I mo...
but...
with y...
Your...
I we...
Craz...
I'm...
Preg...

to...
fre...

ways

rags
of bags

live -
rica

... gone
on lies'

first
he last
earth"
ve
I live -
ca

n nation
blevistation
tion
o ?
rajudice
moonglow
ng, page -
w

live -
rica

Child of the Universe   B♭ - ADF (F?)
2:50 and
Taking it out - 4+

Oh star
Shine on me
I'm just a grain in the universe
I come from the earth
and the earth is a grain
in the galaxy
Could you send some peace on earth
to a child of the universe

Oh sun
There are planets at the top
of the world
And hills and passions
under my feet
Rocks and fish
And worlds I may never see
I only live on earth
I guess I'm just a child of the universe
~~Just a child of the universe~~

Oh moon
I saw your light on
It was gettin' late
Can we talk awhile
You see I lost my smile
I just can't cope
I just can't relate
If you send some peace on earth
send it to a child of the universe
to a child of the universe
~~to your children~~

written "Child in a Universe" on record

Child in a Universe

Oh star
Shine on me
I'm just a grain in the universe
I come from the earth
And the earth is a grain
In the galaxy
Could you send some peace on earth
To a child of the universe

Oh sun
There are planets
At the top of the world
And hills and passions
Under my feet
Rocks and fish
And world I may never see
I only live on earth
I guess I'm just a child of the universe
Just a child of the universe

Oh moon
I saw your light on
It was gettin' late
Can we talk a while
You see I lost my smile
I just can't cope
I just can't relate
If you send some peace on earth
Send it to a child of the universe
To a child of the universe
A child in a universe
Send it to a child in a universe
To your children

Nest

Brown shiny nest
Up in a tree
Maple and warm
Like the nest in me

Wings to fly
Twigs for the nest
Ancient and new
It's a warm address
And I'd like to know
How to give and let live

Eskimo
Did somebody call?
Your name out low
Baby on your back
Oh you're only a woodblock
On the wall

Windy hills
In primal glow rolling
My love lies
In the earth unfolding
And I'd like to know
How to give and let live

Music from love
To make the next bright
Song on a limb
Like a string of light

Just a tree
Brown shiny nest
Ancient and new
It's a hot address

Wind Circles

I dreamed of bells
That Christmas
The plains were bare
The wind blew
In circles
Like a morning fair
Somebody called you
"A drifter playing games"
But by wind circles
The fact remains

You always looked to find
Something you knew
As a child
Some laughter, freedom
In the icy wild
Were you chasing
A blue ribbon
And when you lost it
Were you unsure?
Insecure?
I can see you then
A child in the open blue
Wind circles
Following you

Thru odd jobs
And maintenance
And farms along the reel
Thru living on the edge
And music in the fields
Were you free or poor?
Were you insecure?
You were gentle
All the same

Years before we met
You said you heard
My love call your name

Our love was a Christmas angel
Silently burns
Friends in the sun
Split up
By the trust we never learned

And my eyes are bright
Like my mother's
But this song may be
Purely my own
As I travel lost
In wind circles
Trying to find my home

While you drift
Thru what's happening
A little harder
And never alone
Thru prestige and property
They say a man
Must hold his own
All the lust and confusion
That weighs on the shelf
Wind circles
Send me home to myself
Wind circles
Home to yourself

Mother's Spiritual (1984)

Crazy love

rainbow 4:30
(song of the homeless)

Won

Oh gypsy m
The river ha
our lost m
wit
mo
do
He
sp
sh
wh
th
Cr
M
+
o

Oh star
shine a

Child of the Universe

B♭ - 4DF (F?)
2:50 and
Taking it out - 4+

ways

rags
of rags

This is a song
from the K
The moonli

'Hey mother
Is there m
CAN t
Talk to me
"Well you
brand ne
We are f
We're wr
a note t
Send it .
to Nica
Then do
(don't l
lost in
Oh (send

And this
from the
"We lou
(Sweet a
(Speed f

- But C
C

New m
We bo
To live
freedom
to to
(Sleepy
starri
Good
of Ni
a Bill
(Sent)

ne -
rica

es.
gone
'n lies'

rse

first
e last
aeth"

live -
a

nation
evistation
ion
?
judice
moonglow
g, Page -

live -
a

To a child
(Bill's song)

G - 8DF
3:00, new end - 2:00
= 5:00

Tiny child
you were a miracle to me
A miracle + you will always be
And now that I have such a lot
I'm so tired + my miracle is not

what is life?
Did you read about it in a magazine?
Silent lies
never give you what you need
Is there hope
for a mother + an elf on speed?

Kiss the sun hello
child in the park
make your life a lovin' thing
And I'm so tired.
And you're so wired
And I'm a poet without a poem
and you are my child

"So serene"-
Read about us in a magazine
Then why are we crying by the washing
machine ? →
Let's run away child
And follow a dream
Kiss the sun hello
child in the park
Make your life a lovin' thing
The park is late
The wind is long
The trees have eyes
+ you are my song
my lovely song

what is love?
Child I am here to stand by you
And you will find
your own way, hard + true
And I'll find mine
Cause I'm growing with you
Kiss the sun hello
God + Goddess
make his life a lovin thing
And if I smile
As you reach above
the climbing bars
to see the stars —
You are my love
Child, my love.

To a Child

Tiny child
You were a miracle to me
A miracle
And you will always be
And now that I have such a lot
I'm so tired
And my miracle is not

What is life?
Did you read about it
In a magazine?
Silent lies
Never give you what you need
Is there hope
For a mother and an elf on speed?

Kiss the sun hello
Child in the park
Make your life a lovin' thing
And I'm so tired
And you're so wired
And I'm a poet
Without a poem
And you are my child

"So serene"
Read about us
In a magazine
Then why are we
Crying by the washing machine?
Let's run away child
And follow a dream

Kiss the sun hello
Child in the park

Make your life a lovin' thing
The park is late
The wind is long
The trees have eyes
And you are my song
My lovely song

What is love?
Child I am here to stand by you
And you will find
Your own way
Hard and true
And I'll find mine
'Cause I'm growin' with you.

Kiss the sun hello
God and goddess
Make his life a lovin' thing
And if I smile
As you reach above
The climbing bars
To see the stars
You are my love child
Child my love

We didn't keep in touch. As a matter of fact, I saw her play at the Troubadour, the solo show and that was the inspiration for "Baby, Let's Swing." I didn't even speak to her that evening. The next time I spoke to her was just before starting work on *Mother's Spiritual*.

—TODD RUNDGREN, ARTIST, FAN, AND PRODUCER

The Right to Vote

Thank you sirs
For the right to vote
Bet you didn't know
I had a voice in my throat
Now let's see
Should I vote for 'A' or 'B'?
'A' talks a lot
But not to me
And 'B' wants war
Kill or flunk
Forget the vote
I'll just go out and get drunk

They say a woman's place
Is to wait and serve
Under the veil
Submissive and dear
But I think my place
Is in a ship from space
To carry me
The hell out of here

Patriarchal great religions
Full of angels
Forgiving and fair
While they push the buttons
And blow up the place
(Might as well)
Make room for a worthier race

They say a woman's place
Is to wait and serve
Under the veil
Submissive and dear
But I think my place

Is in a ship from space
To carry me
The hell out of here

All the colors in a race riot
In the land of the free
All the women are on a diet
I'm hungry
Are you hungry
For peace and quiet?

So thank you sirs
For the right to vote
The microwave
And the old mink coat
Now let's see
Should I vote for 'A' or 'B'?
'A' talks a lot
But not to me
And 'B' wants war
Kill or flunk
Forget the vote
I'll just go out and get drunk

They say a woman's place

A Wilderness

Cinnamon hills
Sweet child
And waves of whisper blue
Earth calls to you
Everyday in everyway

Mama's puttin' on some
   warpaint
For a little bit of combat
You ask the reason
You gotta fight for your freedom
Sometimes everyday
In everyway

Many people pass by
Caught up in roles and rules
Many rivers run free
I don't wanna crush
The wilderness in you child
Or the wilderness in me
But how do we keep them both
   alive?
Somehow they must survive
Somehow they must survive
Though there's so much fire
For so little time

We go together
Thru the changing seasons
Hearts of fire
Well you know the world needs
   it
Every day
In every way

Little darlin'
Zap

Touch the earth child
Heaven and earth child

Ahm ahm ahm
Is that a monster?
Yep, no, a crocodile
Ee's eatin' the bed
He's eating the bed?
Yep, ee's eatin' the bed
See im?
Yeah

Ahm ahm ahm
I'm ona eat your...
All bed up
I'm ona eat his...a
Bed all up
I'm ona eat mommy
And bed all up
Ahm ahm ahm

Italics indicates spoken lyrics.

142

Mother's Spiritual, I think, was her favorite record. Although she was a city person, after she got to be 30 or 35, she never liked going into the city as much anymore except to eat. The recording studio scene was really a drag for her. So we built her a studio in her house in Danbury and it was beautiful. At the time it was state of the art, 48 tracks. All the musicians came up there, including John Sebastian, Todd Rundgren, Felix Cavaliere, and Will Lee, who played bass a lot. We had some good times in that studio and that's where *Mother's Spiritual* was made.

— ROSCOE HARRING, LAURA'S SOUND ENGINEER, ROAD MANAGER

Melody in the Sky

I don't know
If this is for a nite
A season or more
I only know
I feel sweet spicy waves
At more shore
Dark and lite
I've been livin' day to day
Nite to nite

Feel this heart beat
No, not cold
Just tired of lies
Evening lites
A melody in the sky

Lover
I'm your friend
And tonite your melody
And you own yourself
I belong to me
Understand
That I've been livin' day to day
Nite to nite

I feel your heart beat
And your kiss can satisfy
Evening lites
Melodies in the sky
Thru the trees they fly
Spring clouds in the park
Rainfall in the dark
Fireflies in our hands
Touching spark to spark
Oh, lovers shine

Lovers forgetting time
Lovers
And truly
You've got your life
Your love
Your life
Your love
I've got mine

And I like you
I'm not waiting
For Miss or Mr. Right
So light our fire
Though my heart's on a wire
Living day to day
Nite to nite
Nite to nite
Nite to nite

Late for Love

Like a sweet gift
From above
Kind of moonlit
And signed with love
Filled with the sweetest
Melt in your mouth thing
You could dream of
People wait
They hesitate
It's getting late

Do you think that love is sex?
Do you think it's security?
Do you give it with vanity
   strings?
Or sailing free?
Do you love a child
Or the wild?
A poem? A tree?
Oh, people wait
They hesitate
It's getting late for love
No, don't be late
For love

Love is really you
Many kinds of love
Is very, really it is you
It's not a Hollywood movie
Love is where you are
Where you are

You could search the mysteries
Of the world
From stars to deep sea pearls

And you could search
The mysteries of the earth
Thru like and death and birth
Just for sweet love

Can you fly it?
Is it made in Japan?

Is it quiet?
Or a ten piece band
Did I have it all at the start?
If love is a child at heart
Do I wait?
Hesitate?
Am I late for love?
No, I can't be late
For love

Love is really you

Many kinds of
Love is very
Really it is you
It's not a Hollywood movie
Love is where you are

Here is a story of Laura, our pal, the character. My wife and I were having her over. She came by and by then we felt like we knew each other forever. I was still surprised when she said "I think I'd like to take a nap." I said, "Sure Laura, we've got a guest room up there with a TV and whatever." She said, "No, I think I'd really like to have my nap in your bed." I was so thrown and God bless my wife, Catherine goes, "Well, sure Laura, it's right at the top of the stairs." And Laura had herself a nice little nap and then got up and we went about our business. I considered it a gesture of intimacy and one that I appreciated.

—JOHN SEBASTIAN, ARTIST AND FRIEND

Free Thinker

You don't have your own
You're livin' thru others
Toss and turn at night
But you play it demure
And what's more
You don't think you've got the right
To be a free thinker
You could give yourself the right
You could shine your special light

Are you a consumer
A mere number
On a supermarket line?
Wear a perfect mask
And never show your feelings
Maybe you can make the time
To be a free thinker
You could find your own style
You may feel more alive

Do you ever wonder
Can we save our planet
And where will it go in time?
While hawks* destroy
And healers send joy
Back to the starry nite line
For a free thinker
With some individuality
You may find you feel more free

*This word is being used in its traditional sense of war
consciousness, and not in reference to the spirit of the soaring bird.

Man in the Moon

Man in the moon
I ran past my home
To your shore
To melt the arctic heat
In my breast
Next to yours
It was just my fantasy
For a real world

What do you hear?
What is it we really share?
Do you know the depth
Of my need and my prayer
Or is it just my fantasy
For a new world
It's true
You'll see it baby
There's a new world
Comin' thru

Is it just fine for us to live
In a world that cannot give?
As for me I know I'm strong
And I belong
In a new world
You'll see
You'll see it baby
There's a new world in me
If you want me
You'll find me in a new world
I want love, respect and power
To make a new world

I wanna raise my babies
In a new world

Give them peace and happiness
You know you're the old world
And I'm the new world
It's true
You'll see it baby
The new world

Man in the moon

Talk to a Green Tree

Baby in the cradle
I need to stay strong
I need some ease
Before long
And all the world around me
Is still in love with war
And I must teach that baby
That love is what life is for

And you may help me
Pretty daddy
But you can never lead me
'Cause you don't seem to hear
  me
Gonna talk to a green tree
Talk to a green tree
Green tree
What am I gonna do?
What am I gonna do?
I'm a working woman
With a baby on my back
Won't you see me thru

Wind in the treetops
Flame in the song
Mother I need your wise words
But you died before he was born
And all the world around me
Is still in love with war
And I must teach that baby,
  momma
That love is
What life is for

And you have fire
Little child
And we are growing
And I could really fly
With you by the green tree
We'll lie by the green tree
Green tree
We're your company
We're your company
I'm a working woman
With a baby on my back
I need some energy

Listen pretty daddy
You can take my place
Childcare and home
Is no disgrace
But eight days a week
May wilt your wild flower
And after you've done it all
Big daddy
Be ready for the midnite hour

And you, society
You can never lead me
'Cause you don't seem to hear
  me
Gonna talk to a green tree
Talk to a green tree
Green tree
What am I gonna do
To set my spirit free?
I'm a working woman
With a baby on my back
I need some energy

Trees of the Ages

Trees of the ages
You stroll past them
They toss, shimmer in the wind
You stroll by them
You won't outlast them
They know everything
Hello, hello
Trees of the ages
Evergreen
Hello, hello, only you
Can keep my peaceful dreams

Sweep of the trees
Energy spirals
Co-existing in a glow
Believe in a tree
Trees know what every
Zen master needs to know
Hello, hello
Trees of the evening
And the dawn
Hello, hello
So good to those who stroll along

It is known
In special circles
Tree elves guide the way
High above
What people break
Elves rebuild each day
Oh they live in strange places
Magic traces
In trees of the ages
The green love in the world

Strollin' at ease
In the great green harmonies

The Brighter Song

You are a free woman
You understand the earth
You say you want an end to
    violence
Feel safe in the universe
Sister believe
You are stronger brighter
Your dream's a little wilder
Sister believe
Sister believe in your happiness

You are a green peace dreamer
You understand the earth
You say you want to save the sea
And skies of the universe
Sister believe
You are stronger, wilder
Your moon's a little brighter
Sister believe
Sister believe in your happiness

Sweet and shining dreams
They burn
And your light
Shine it free and bright
And if the world can't see it
Give it to the wild night

You are a romantic woman
Sweet and rare
You are young
And you are old
Black and white
You're everywhere
Sister believe

You are stronger, wilder
Your moon's a little brighter
Sister believe
Sister believe in your happiness
Don't forget your happiness

Roadnotes

Gypsy fever
I've been here many times
The motels
The trailers
The netted tents
Of the road
I've been on these lands
Thru space time
In my own time
On my own time baby
Independently wanting you
I've been wanting you
Wanting you
Wanting to
What's a woman to do now?
Lover
That's right

Me and my friends
Somewhere on the road
Child and dog play
Winds they blow
And blow
Happy birthday thirties
What do I want?
My candles glow
Baby I want everything
Just everything
I want everything
That you can bring
'Cause my heart needs to sing
   now
Lover
That's right lover

You are here
Music in my ear
A wild dear
A magic potion
Hold me tight
Angel of the night
Hold me right
'Cause my love is the ocean
Give you everything
Just everything
I want everything
That you can bring
To set the night in motion
Lover that's right, lover that's
   right
Music of the night
I hear music of the night
And I'm here lovin' you
Baby I'm lovin' you
Baby I'll be lovin' you
Baby I've been lovin' you
Lovin' you, yes

Sophia

Sophia
Goddess of wisdom
And dream
Shine your light
Shine your light
For a gypsy queen
In a midnite dream

Sophia
Goddess of wisdom
Serene
Shine your light
Shine your light
For a gypsy queen
In a midnite dream

Hecate, queen of the night
Queen of the bold
Shine your light
Down the open road
Midnight in my eyes
Highway in my hair
I don't want no diamond rings
I don't want no pretty things
I'm lookin' for the highway
To my soul

Sophia
Goddess of wisdom
And dream
Shine your light
Shine your light
For a gypsy queen
In a midnite dream

Sophia
Goddess of wisdom
Serene
Shine your light
Shine your light
For a gypsy queen
In a midnite dream

Hecate, queen of the night
Queen of the bold
Women want to change the
    world
Make it whole
Midnite in my eyes
Highway in my hair
I don't want no diamond rings
I got all my pretty things
I'm lookin' for the highway
To my soul

Sophia
Goddess of wisdom
And dream
Shine your light
Shine your light
For a gypsy queen
In a midnite dream

Laura told me the album *Mother's Spiritual* was as close as possible to her artistic vision. It was near perfect, 95 percent there.

— PATTY DILAURIA, FRIEND

Mother's Spiritual

On a street corner
Where the kids boogie all nite
Or where the winds sing
And the stars shine
Like holiday lites
Come a band of angels
Salvation in their might
And as for peace on earth...
Feel this love
My brothers and sisters
Feel the season turn
She is the mother of time
Wonders that take you
Rivers that give
That's where mother's spiritual
   lives

Come to the lites my sisters
And take what you need
Doesn't matter my brothers
Your Sunday creed
'Cause each one's a lover
To this winter nite star
A pilgrim, a pioneer
That's who you are
Feel this love
My brothers and sisters
Feel the season turn
She is the mother of time
It's not war
It's life she gives
And that's where mother's
   spiritual lives

Talk of a ruby love
Lovers share
Find your love
Lose your love
Here and there
So you go home
Do your own thing
And the ocean sings to me
That love is always alive
And part of thee
Feel this love
My brothers and sisters
Feel the season turn
She is the mother of time
Light and darkness
Come to her kiss
'Cause that's where mother's
   spiritual lives

Refrain

What is life?
Did you read about it
In a magazine?

Love is really you

Dedicated to the trees

Live At The Bottom Line (1990)

Roll of the Ocean

I want the roll
The roll of the ocean
I want the roll
The roll of the ocean
I want the sweet deep
Elemental roll

I want Coltrane in the moon
Just that starry aching tune
Will do
I only want the news
From the heavenly muse

I want the roll
The roll of the ocean
I want the roll
The roll of the ocean
I want the sweet complete
Elemental roll

Oh star up in the tree
Ready now
I will set the mystery free
I only want the news
From the heavenly muse

Free me
From a world that is so very
Hard and cold
I am your visionary
I want talk in musk
Passion in the rain
Peace on earth
What can I say?
I'm an angel

What can I say?
I'm a woman
I want the roll
The roll of the ocean
I want the sweet deep
Elemental roll
I want the roll

Companion

I don't wanna marry
I don't want your money
But love's come our way
Just a warm companion
Is what I want honey

Life is complicated
Funny
Love can be that way
When just a warm companion
Is what I want honey
A very special trust
A very special lust

Walk inside the rain
Laughter in the dark
That lovin'
Lovin'
Spark
Like the sky above me
Like a bird born to sing
Harmony
Is what I want honey
A very special trust

Wild World

Dinner in the kitchen
Delicious to eat
Thou shall not kill darlin'
Let wild things run free
I heard
The wolf is gone
I heard
So is the whale of the sea
And who are we?
Where are we goin'
To be so willin'
For the killin'
Of the wild world?

Animals
Trapped by man's endangered
    soul
By science, sport and fashion
I heard
The wolf is gone
The baby seal
Sister whose back
Does that fur belong on?
And who are you?
Where are you goin'
To be so willin'
For the killin'
Of the wild world?

Consumer blindness
I'm givin' it up
Consider compassion
When you're livin' it up
Wild world
Wild world

Oh it's all around you
Wild world

Park Song

Let your leaf fall
In my child's hand
He's laughin' and whirlin'
His love is a ten piece band
That child throws sparks
Across the park
Across this whole crazy world
Ooh
If that were his lovin' plan

Autumn leaves
Drift by like angels
Drift past the world
Of man made reality
"They" call "great"
But I couldn't relate it
From the start
So cool the tired
Renew the weary
As you float down
In wonder

To a child   G - BDF
Child of the Universe   B♭ - ADF (F?)   00 new end - 2:00
2:50 and   = 5 :00
Taking it out - 4+   is be
                                          a lot
                                          is not

1978 ~

Oh star
Shine on me
I'm just a atom in the universe
I come

Broken Rainbow   4:30
(song of the homeless)

The old people of the earth
tell stories
An old woman of the old ways
She said " I recall my joy
in better days".

The young warriors
of the open rainbow
said " tell me is it true?
Tell me - do some live out of rags
and bags in the citys too?
Is it true?"

At the edge where I live
At the very edge where I live —
Home sweet home America

The earth ones
they said 'Our religion
is in these lands and skies.
Sweet mother — Our land's gone
to modern worlds , modern lies'

The earth ones
and the new ecology
' You know we were the first
Believe me we will be the last
to keep the light for the earth"
At the edge where I live
At the very edge where I live —
Home sweet home America

Native American nation
Caught in the devistation
endless situation
what can I do ?
The ghost of prejudice
cuts thru the moonglow
Poet on a crying page —
' Broken Rainbow"

At the edge
At the very edge where I live —
home sweet home America

Broken Rainbow

The old people of the earth
Tell stories
An old woman
Of the old ways
She said – "I recall my joy
In better days"

The young warriors
Of the open rainbow
Said, "Tell me is it true,
Tell me, Do some live
Out of bags and rags
In the cities too?
Is it true?"

At the edge where I live
At the very edge where I live
Home sweet home America

The earth ones
They said, "Our religion
Is in these lands and skies
Sweet mother
Our land's gone
To modern worlds
Modern lies"

The earthways
And the new ecology
You know we were the first
Believe me
We will be the last
To keep a light for the earth
At the edge where I live

At the very edge where I live
Home sweet home America

Native American nation
Caught in the devastation
An endless situation
What can I do?
The ghost of prejudice
Cuts thru the moonglow
Poet on a cryin' page
Broken Rainbow

Home sweet home
America

1978 ✓   Key-G 80F
Crazy love   To a child.   G - 8UT
(bill's song)   3:00 new end-2:00
Oh gypsy man   } Tiny child   = 5:00
The gypsy man. } re'll were a miracle to me

Child of the Universe B♭-ADF (F?)   Broken Rainbow 7:30
                                      (of the homeless)

Oh star
Shine on me
I'm just a grain
I come from the
and the earth
In the galaxy
Could you send
to a child of

Oh sun
There are plan
of the world
And hills and
under my fee
Rocks and fi
And worlds
I only live o
I guess I'm
~~just a chil~~

Oh moon
I saw you
It was get
Can we to
You see I
I just ca
I just ca
If you se
send it
to a chi
~~to your chi~~

written

Women of the One World

This is a song
from the keepers of the light
The moonlight

Hey mother—
Is there milk inside the night
(All the creatures of the night)
Talk to me!

"Well you—well you're just brand new
brand new
We are fighting against great odds
We're writing
a note to the stars
Send it — send it
to Nicaragua
Then down to South Africa
(don't let it get)
lost in America
Oh (send it) In the rainbow mail to one world

And this is a song
from the mothers of the moon
"We love you—
(Sweet dreams babies)
(speed peace + freedom soon)

—But (cause) you—well you're just brand
(you're like a brand new moon) new
New moon
We bore you   (Our visions-protect your
To live not die   (true freedom + take
freedom—   back the nite)
to touch the sky
(sleepy)   To live + let live
Starry Lullaby
Goodnite children
If Nicaragua
a note
all thru South Africa
(Sent) from America

We oppose all war
We affirm all life
We are scared + outraged
But we are hopeful
Because we are love
Rain wind star fire
As our witness

We are dancers
sweepers
+ bookeepers
We take you to movies
or parks or for walks on talks
By rain wind star + fire
This is an ever loving love song
to you
from the women of the one world

of the earth
of the old ways
my joy

ow
it true?
live out of ~~bags~~ rags
city-too?

I live
here, I live —
e America

ion
and skies.
land's gone
modern lies'

gy
e the first
be the last
the earth"
I live
here, I live —
merica

erican nation
the devastation
uation
I do?
f prejudice
the moonglow
rying page—
bow

e I live—
merica

Dancers Sweepers Bookkeepers
(Women of the One World)

Songs come
From the mothers of the moon
Goodnight children
We are dancers
Sweepers
Bookkeepers
We take you to the movies

For walks and talks
Thru rain, wind, sun, star
Women of the one world
We oppose war
Women of the one world
Dancers sweepers bookkeepers
We take you to the movies
Take you to the movies
Women of the one world
One world

She loved playing "Japanese Restaurant." She had fun with that every night. Laura was very careful about putting the show together so that everything was enjoyable. We started with "The Wind" every night. That was her way in. It wasn't like we would change the set list. The set had a life of its own. You couldn't do it out of order. It was complete from front to back, including her encores, which were solos. We had worked on "Love on a Two-Way Street"— maybe she even recorded it. "Heebee Jeebee" we worked on. Mostly soul classics. She liked the Delfonics and the Dells. I remember her particularly loving to do "Love on a Two-Way Street." If she liked a song she could make it her own, which is something very few people can do. How many people thought she wrote some of the covers she did. She owns "Up on the Roof."

—JIMMY VIVINO, GUITARIST AND LAURA NYRO BANDLEADER

The Japanese Restaurant Song

We went to a Japanese restaurant
The dogs, the kids and me
Loose my cares
In a cup of plum wine
And salads from The sea
We tripped into the calm little room
With the sliding paper walls
Mom was wearin' her rose kimono
She was waiting for the fall

Just another nite
A day in the life
Just another foreign film
In black and white
When you mess with them
You're out of the realm of Zen
When they put on their party hats
The cook cracked

Don't you know
It's just another nite
A day in the life
Just another foreign film
In black and white
When you mess with them
You're beyond the realm of Zen
When they put on their party hats
The cook cracked

The cook, he told me —
"Children not exactly well behaved"
I said "Well you can't have it all"
And really who cares
When the magic plum wine
Is dancing on the paper walls
Then your lover shows up
Puts a sweet hello on your lips
And your transported
To the mist on the mountain
Till everyone runs in for the kiss

As the wine descended
My citizenship surrendered
And I became a geisha
I moved thru the mystery
Dark and content
With a radical feminist bent
Mr. Cook Don't you save my life
Don't you save my love
I am quite contented yes sir
The elders say
They'll be grown and gone someday
So lets enjoy the adventure
I'm sorry
but it's just another nite
A day in the life
I'm sorry
but it's just another nite

Japanese Restaurant

We went to a Japanese restaurant
The dogs, the kids and me
Lose my cares
In a cup of plum wine
And salads from the sea
We tripped into the calm little
  room
With the sliding paper wails
Mom was wearin' her rose
  kimono
She was waiting for the fall

Just another nite
A day in the life
Just another foreign film
In black and white
When you mess with them
You're out of the realm of Zen
When they put on their party
  hats
The cook cracked

The cook, he told me
"Children not exactly well
  behaved"
I said "Well you can't have it all"
And really who cares
When the magic plum wine
Is dancing on the paper walls
Then your lover shows up
Puts a sweet hello on your lips
And you're transported
To the mist on the mountain
'Til everyone runs in for the kiss

Don't you know
It's just another nite
A day in the life
Just another foreign film
In black and white
When you mess with them
You're beyond the realm of Zen
When they put on their party
  hats
The cook cracked

As the wine descended
My citizenship surrendered
And I became a geisha
I moved through the mystery
Dark and content
With a radical feminist bent
Mr. Cook don't you save my life
Don't you save my love
I am quite contented, yes sir
The elders say
Kids are grown and gone
  someday
So lets enjoy the adventure
I'm sorry
But it's just another nite
A day in the life
I'm sorry
But it's just another nite

Walk The Dog And Light The Light (1993)

She didn't really tour around albums. It wasn't like that with her. She would rather write songs and stay at home. She didn't like touring. She enjoyed performing. People at the Bottom Line will attest to that. That's where her best shows were. Songwriting was work for Laura. Did it relax her and put her in a different state? Not really. It was work and she loved to work. It was her dangling participles and her little fragments from here and there, and she would try to join them all together.

—ROSCOE HARRING, LAURA'S SOUND ENGINEER, ROAD MANAGER

A Woman of the World

There's peace of mind
Now that I draw the line
Will you be runnin'
Out of fools
My love's got new rules
This time

Because friends and lovers
Could give the sun
To each other
Not this rain
I was a foolish girl
Now I'm a wornan
Of the world

Wisdom be mine
It's been a hard lesson
But I'm movin' up in school
Where you learn
To play it cool
And I just know this time

That friends and lovers
Could give the sun
To each other
Not this pain
I was a foolish girl
Now baby
I'm a woman of the world
A woman of the world
I'm free, free, free
My love's no competition
It's about...harmony

Sweet harmony
I'll take my dream
Into the future
I'd only bring it back again
This time as friends

Friends and lovers
Who give the sun
To each other
Not this rain
If I was a foolish girl
Baby now
I'm a woman of the world

We had a very balanced group. We had three men and three women. It was such a great group because of the way she put it together. I questioned a lot of things at first and then understood them. Things like having to have a female bass player or having to have a certain number of women and a certain number of men. I never thought in those terms for any other project I approached. But I understood for Laura that was a balance, nature; it was correct, it was right. It's the first time I saw anybody hire in terms of sexual balance, to make the group completely equal. It was important because her music required human relationships in the players. Every aspect of her songs were her.

—JIMMY VIVINO, GUITARIST AND LAURA NYRO BANDLEADER

The Descent of Luna Rosé

(Dedicated to my period)
Lighten up
Baby
On my love
Lighten up
Like summer and ices
And stars above

This month'll soon be gone
These blues linger on
It's the time of the month

So lighten up
Baby
Tonite
Tell me a joke
Make sure it's funny
By the bedroom lite

Baby don't look at me
Like Freud
That could create a void
And get you thrown out
My love
'Cause every day
I'm waiting for Luna Rosé

I've been waiting
For Luna Rosé to descend
To bring it on again
These blues are serious
I feel delirious

Ooh yeah d-d-d-d dip
Lighten up baby

Ooh yeah
This month'll soon be gone
These blues linger on
And every day
I'm waiting for Luna Rosé
Waiting for Luna Rosé
I'm waiting for Luna Rosé

We dealt with each song totally as a separate entity. Each song, from one orchestration to another, was dealt with individually. Laura is the glue that ties them all together.

—GARY KATZ, CO-PRODUCER, *WALK THE DOG & LIGHT THE LIGHT*

Art of Love

Celebrate the holiday
Life is for givin'
You belong
To the livin'
Sister
Brother
Are we born to learn
The art of love?
Heart and soul
Body and mind
Mother earth
To stars above

Oh
Happy holiday
With love

Shelter from the storm
There but for fortune
You and I belong
To one world
One address S.O.S.

Hear that love message
All around the world
"Love not war
Let peace shine for
Every boy and girl"
Child with a dove
Vision of
A happy holiday
With love

"Peace on earth from Tibet"
"Peace on earth from Iraq"

"Peace on earth from Israel"
"From Africa,"
"From Jamaica"
"From America,"
"From Cuba"
"Peace on earth from Italy"

Sister
Brother
Are we born to learn
The art of love?
Love not war
Let peace shine for
The earth
Child with a dove
Vision of
A happy holiday
Happy holiday with love

Lite a Flame

In the zoo
They gave him a cage
Circus put a sparkle
On his face
Away from life
The elephant walks
Shadow across a dream
Lost for ivory

Oh freedom
Lite a flame

It's like prejudice
For the color of your skin
Prejudice for a woman
Prejudice for an animal
Like the elephant
Of the plain

Masai moon
In the morningrise
Africa –
The world comes alive
A matriarch
Leads the tribe
To the sweet water
The cool feelin'
And the way to survive

Oh freedom
Lite a flame

It's like prejudice
For the color of your skin
Prejudice for a woman

Prejudice for an animal
Like the elephant
Of the plain

Of the plain
For greed not need
Societies sleep
Lead the killing hand on

Young ones
Full of spark
A wave of birds
Across the park
Kids climbing
Sliding, riding free
Elephant child hiding
Behind a tree

Prejudice
For an animal
Like the elephant
Of the plain

Louise's Church

(For the sculptor Louise Nevelson, musician Billie Holiday, painter Frida Kahlo and artists of inspiration)

Sappho was a poet
Billie was a real musician
Frida drew the moon
I'm goin' by
Louise's Church
She built in the city
Art of grace and style
That could make me smile
Talk to me
Goddess of life and music
Shine on me awhile

Sappho was a poet
Billie was a real musician
Frida drew the moon
The candle at
Louise's Church
Lite it for your vision
For the changes
To save the planet of ages
Talk to us
Heavenly Muse
Shine on us awhile

(And for the next wave of feminism)

Every moment you are working in the studio with her music, her fingerprints are all over it, her palm prints or footprints. She was highly professional and very comfortable in the studio, although very sensitive about her work and meticulous—something I can relate to.

—GARY KATZ, CO-PRODUCER, *WALK THE DOG AND LIGHT THE LIGHT*

Walk the Dog and Light the Light

Gonna make my livin'
Independence
Workin' with the gypsies
They call it
'That ribbon of highway'
Gonna buy a house
Make it a home
Another mile
A shot of coffee
Take my sugar
On the phone

"Child of mine
I'm headin' for the city line
Oo, walk the dog
And light the light
I'll see you Sunday
'Cause I'm workin' on
Saturday nite"

They make their livin'
Their independence
Dawn thru moonlight
On both sides
Of that ribbon of highway
A melting pot
They come from all over
Thru down south
Pacific rim
Northern snow
And east thru autumn
Are you fine?
My love
Mama's headin'
For the city line

Oo, run the dog
Darlin' light the light
I'll see you Sunday
'Cause I'm workin' on
Saturday nite

See you Sunday, 'cause
I'm workin' on Saturday
Nite

Operator
Take this precious dime
Precious time
Mama's headed for the city
The city, the city line

Oo, in my heart
I will light the light

And see you Sunday
'Cause I'm workin'
On Saturday nite

See you Sunday
'Cause I'm singin'
On Saturday
N-i-t-e

Angel In The Dark (2001)

Angel in the Dark

Angel
Of
My heart
Come back to me
Angel
Whoa
In the dark
So I can see
'Cause I can't live no more
Without an angel
Of love, so if you hear

Come back to me, come back
Come back to me, come back
Answer my prayer
Come back to me, come back
Come back to me, come back
Answer my prayer

Angel
Hear my song
Because the night's so long
Come back to me
I don't know how
I don't know where
I'll be dreamin' and on my feet
  again
'Cause I can't laugh no more
Without an angel
So if you're there

Come back to me, come back
Come back to me, come back
Answer my prayer
Come back to me, come back

Come back to me, come back
Answer my prayer

Answer my prayer
I can't laugh no more
Without an angel
So if you're there

Come back to me, come back
Come back to me, come back
Answer my prayer
Answer

Come back to me, come back
Come back to me, come back
Answer my prayer

Come back to me, come back
Come back to me, come back

Triple Goddess Twilight

I was a sweet baby in my
    mother's arms
We were strollin' through the
    park
Picnic
Peace walk
Progress
Just a baby in her arms
My politics are based on her
    charms

Triple Goddess Twilight
Slow down
Feel the land
Violet everywhere
I'll meet you there

Mother, you died young and left
    me
Your twilight colors
Rosé
Ah burgundy
Coral mist
What are the shades of loneliness

Triple Goddess Twilight
Late sky violet and pink
All roads lead to Venus
I'll meet you there
In your dream of progress

My grandfather painted houses
On a ladder in the sky
He was working class
Urbane

Street-wise
Said, "We can change the world
    girl
Love will inspire,"
Told me this through whiskey
And revolutionary fire

Triple Goddess Twilight
Last trace of ruby and flame
First star leads to Venus

He left a war
To walk in peace now
Said life was for
Our dream
Our dream of progress

When I first met her, she had me come up to her house in Connecticut—the big house she turned into a recording studio. And there was a little cottage that she lived in—very Spartan: Japanese bed on the floor, piano, her dog Ember, and no TV. Her only playback system was a child's pink and purple walkman thing. There was no professional recording equipment where she lived. She had the state-of-the-art studio up the hill. For listening and working at home there was just this toy playback unit which was great. It had little speakers. It was something you would buy at Kids R Us.

—JIMMY VIVINO, GUITARIST AND LAURA NYRO BANDLEADER

Sweet Dream Fade

Do you wanna make a sweet
   dream fade
After all the tries we made
Never mind perfection
Heroes or heroines
Tonight
Let's be lovers again
Tonight
Lover let's be friends
Or make a sweet dream

Too many tears can dim the light
Give or take
Wrong or right
Innovation
Make amends
Tonight
Let's be lovers again
Tonight
Lover let's be friends
Or make a sweet dream fade

Kids cry
Money flies away
Dream on baby, dream on
Where have all the years gone?

Do you wanna make a sweet
   dream fade
After all the sweet tries we made
Never mind perfection
Heroes or heroines
Tonight
Let's be lovers again

Tonight
Oo, baby

Lover let's be friends
Lover let's be friends
Or make a sweet dream fade
Lover let's be friends
Lover let's be friends
Or make a sweet dream fade
Lover let's be friends
Or make a sweet dream fade

Serious Playground

I walk the path
Of heart and soul
I make my living
Building homes
I build them out of music
With my imagination
Sound architectural tools I use
My boss is
The Muse

Serious playground
I'm down for the music
Of my life
Serious playground
Day or night
I walk the path
Of heart and soul
I try to make a living
Of my own
Out of music with celebration
Sound architecture and rose and
    blues
My boss is
The Muse

Serious playground
That's where I work and play
Serious playground
Night or day

More
More than stress or strain
More
More than just capital gain

So send me the music
Like wings to fly
Natural high

Serious playground
I'm down for the music
Of my life
Serious playground
Here for the music
Here for the music
Serious playground
For the music
Of my life

Serious playground
Here for the music
Of my life
Serious playground
I'm here for the music
Of my life

Gardenia Talk

Gardenia talk
It's spring
Gardenia talk
It must be spring
Oh oh oh oh

Maybe
I'd like to know you
Struck by the poetry
I know it's not the time to show
    you
I may know you in my dream

You never hear me
Talk the talk
Talk the talk of love
Swoon like a teenager
Oh
Gardenia talk, oo oo oo
Gardenia talk, oo oo oo
Are you just some sweet stranger

I only met you on the bus to
    springtime
Now I'm struck by a fantasy
If there's something I can do
With this dream
Fills the darkness like the sea

That's where I heard you
Talk the talk
Talk the talk of love
Swoon like a teenager
Oh
Gardenia talk, oo oo oo

Gardenia talk, oo oo oo
Am I just some sweet stranger

Gardenia talk

It's spring
Gardenia talk
It must be spring
Gardenia talk
Meltin' everything

Oo la la la oo oo oo
Oo la la la oo oo oo

Are you just
Are you just
Are you just some sweet stranger
Oo la la la oo oo oo
Oo la la la oo oo oo
Gardenia talk, oo oo oo
Gardenia talk, oo oo oo

Animal Grace

Of the animal question
Animal grace
I love my dog
I rest my case

Oh Saint Francis
Held them dear
Bird at the fountain
I see out there

We need a change of mind
This earth is
An interspecies affair
Affair
Interspecies affair

Don't Hurt Child

Don't hurt child
I know you do
I was young and wild once too
Let the summer storm
Clear the sky
When you cry

Don't hurt child
You need to find your way
In the madness of the day
And if it don't break you
It will be
Your song

May the love that we know
Keep us strong
Don't hurt child

Baby comes into the world
In a veil of divine love
Gets caught up in thunder and rain
What were you dreamin' of
Don't

Don't hurt child
I took my stand
But the key is in your hand
Heal your wild wing
And fly

May the love that you know
Get you by
Don't hurt
My baby child

CODA

Here's your old friendship ring
I can't wear it no more
Here's your old love letters
I can't read 'em anymore

Love you've gone from me
And left behind
So many memories

Here's your old teddy bear
That you won for me
At the state fair
Here's more lingering love
It's in my heart and it's tearing it apart

Love you've gone from me
Left behind
So many memories

PERMISSIONS

All words and music written solely by Laura Nyro. Notice of publisher is given, followed by the year of copyright.

INDEX

127 American Dreamer
37 And When I Die
186 Angel in the Dark
192 Animal Grace
179 Art of Love
97 Beads of Sweat
92 Been on a Train
21 Billy's Blues
91 Blackpatch
25 Blowin' Away
151 Brighter Song, The
166 Broken Rainbow
88 Brown Earth
34 Buy and Sell
23 California Shoeshine Boys
73 Captain for Dark Mornings
83 Captain Saint Lucifer
107 Cat Song
133 Child in a Universe
102 Children of the Junks
99 Christmas in My Soul
194 CODA
161 Companion
66 Confession, The
126 Crazy Love
167 Dancers Sweepers Bookkeepers
     (Women of the One World)
63 December Boudoir
177 Descent of Luna Rose, The
193 Don't Hurt Child
50 Eli's Comin'
57 Emmie
29 Flim Flam Man
147 Free Thinker
191 Gardenia Talk
78 Gibsom Street
28 Goodbye Joe
33 He's a Runner
105 I Am the Blues
32 I Never Meant to Hurt You
170 Japanese Restaurant
145 Late for Love
27 Lazy Susan
130 Light-Pop's Principle
180 Lite a Flame
48 Lonely Women
181 Louise's Church
43 Lu
41 Lucky
148 Man in the Moon
81 Man Who Sends Me Home
96 Map to the Treasure

144 Melody in the Sky
75 Mercy on Broadway
109 Midnite Blue
103 Money
114 Morning News
155 Mother's Spiritual
119 Mr. Blue (The Song of
     Communications)
124 My Innocence
134 Nest
85 New York Tendaberry
61 Once It Was Alright Now
     (Farmer Joe)
163 Park Song
47 Poverty Train
156 Refrain
121 Rhythm and Blues
141 Right to Vote, The
152 Roadnotes
160 Roll of the Ocean
77 Save the Country
190 Serious Playground
110 Smile
153 Sophia
128 Springblown
54 Stoned Soul Picnic
     (Picnic, A Green City)
31 Stoney End
106 Stormy Love
45 Sweet Blindness
189 Sweet Dream Fade
82 Sweet Lovin' Baby
129 Sweet Sky
149 Talk to a Green Tree
80 Time and Love
51 Timer
139 To a Child
74 Tom Cat Goodbye
150 Trees of the Ages
187 Triple Goddess Twilight
93 Upstairs by a Chinese Lamp
183 Walk the Dog and Light the Light
19 Wedding Bell Blues
90 When I Was a Freeport and You
     Were the Main Drag
162 Wild World
142 Wilderness, A
135 Wind Circles
175 Woman of the World, A
59 Woman's Blues
71 You Don't Love Me When I Cry

ABOUT THE CD ACCOMPANYING THIS BOOK

THE INTERVIEW

Following the diagnosis of her illness, Laura very much wanted to express the meaning of music in her life for posterity. Her partner, Maria, a painter, was to become her videographer.

Maria, devastated by the diagnosis and desperately seeking some hopeful course of action for Laura, kept postponing the project feeling that the illness deserved complete attention. Finally—and this was not much later because treatment began quickly—Laura put her foot down. This was what she wanted, she said, and did she have to hire someone to help her with it? It wasn't an entreaty, but an ultimatum.

Laura always knew what she wanted in life and never more so than when life became ever more precious. The words you will hear come from that creative collaboration between the poet and the painter.

—PATTY DILAURIA, LAURA AND MARIA'S FRIEND

THE SONGS

It was 1966 in New York. I think we were at Milt Okun's office. Laura must have been 18. She was enormously talented. This was probably our second meeting and we asked her to play some more songs. She was nervous. At one point I wanted to see if she knew anybody else's songs, which I admit in Laura's biography by Michelle Kort that it was stupid of me to ask. The next step was, I went out and got Jerry Schoenbaum to sign her and we recorded what became *More Than a New Discovery* for Verve/Forecast. What you have on this disc are two of the songs Laura played for us that day, and the earliest known recordings of "And When I Die" and "Lazy Susan."

—ARTIE MOGUL, MUSIC PUBLISHER

get yourself clean
from the sugar daddy con
no sugar daddy
no con

money so
mundane
capital crime
immoral
assembly line
capital crime

No money

Can turn me
around

they'd
kill you
on the
assembly line

a turn off the sound

in my serious playground

Man in the moon
I ran past my home
to your shore
to melt the arctic heat
in my breast
next to yours
It was just my fantasy
for a real world

what do you hear?
what is it we really share?
Do you know the depth of my need
+ my prayer?

Or is it just my fantasy
for a new world
It's true - you'll see it baby
there's a new world - comin thru

As for me
I know I'm strong
+ I belong
in a new world
You'll see
You'll see it baby
there's a new world in me
I want peace for
my children
new world
new world

mamas puttin on some
warpaint
for a little bit of combat
You ask the reason
You gotta fight for your freedom
Sometimes every day
in every way
Many people pass by
Caught up in roles + rules
Many of us are free
I don't want to crush
the wilderness in you child
or the wilderness in me
But how do we keep them
both alive somehow
they must survive

I belong to time
he changed my face
I'm a fine one timer
We got me walkin
the gates of space
Keep re remembering
doors that I use to
walk thru
I'm not tryin
to talk you down
I could walk
them doors
a pleasure ground
was sweet + funny
pleasure ground
I know about
money
+ know about
Time

Sweet blindness
Down by the grapevine
drink my daddy's wine
of wonder - wonder
oh sweet blindness
a little magic
a little kindness

Is it just fine for us to live
In a world that cannot give
As for me I know I'm strong

If you want me you'll find me
in a new world
I want love respect + power
to make a new world
I wanna raise my babies
in a new world
Give them peace + happiness

Broken Rainbow

You know you're the old world
+ I'm the new world
It's true
You'll see it baby
The new world
man in the moon

The old people of the earth
tell stories
an old woman
of the old ways
she said 'I recall my joy
in better days'

The young warriors
of the open rainbow
said tell me is it true
Tell me - Do some live
out of bags + rags.
In the cities too
Is it true?'
At the edge where I live
at the very edge where I live
Home sweet home
America

They said:
Your religion
is in the land + sky
Sweet Mother
Our land's gone
to modern worlds
modern lies

The earth ways
+ the new ecology
You know we where
the first
believe me
We will be the last
the keep a life
for the earth
At the edge where
I live
At the very edge
where I live
Home sweet home America

Native American nation
Caught in the Devistation
An endless education
what can I do?
The ghost of prejudice
cuts thru the moonglow
Foot on a cryin page
Broken Rainbow
at the edge where I live
home sweet home America

Jap Rest song

Jap Rest song
We went to a Jap Rest
The dogs the kids + me
loose my cares
in a cup of phem wine
+ something from the sea
We turned into
the calm little room
with the sliding paper walls
Mom was wearin
her rose kimono
She was waiting for the fall

Just another night
a day in the life
Just another magic trick
in black + white
when you mess with them
You're out of the realm
of zen
when they put on their
party hats
the cook cracked

The cook he told me
Children not exactly well behaved
I said well you cant have it all
+ really who cares
when the magic plum wine
is dancin on the paper walls
Then your lover shows up
Puts a sweet hello on your L
+ your transported
to the mist on the mountain
til everyone runs in for the tea

don't you know
it's just another nite
a day in the life
Just another foreign film
in black + white
when you mess with
them
You're beyond the realm of
when they put on their
party hats
the cooked cracked

As the wine descended
My citizenship surrendered
+ I became a geisha women
I moved thru the mystery
hack + content
with a radical feminist bent
Mr Cook
don't you save my life
No don't you save my love
I am quite contented
Yes Sir
The elders say
they'll be good grown
+ gone someday
So let's enjoy the adventure
I'm sorry
but it's just another nite
a day in the life . . . .

where quakers
+ revolutionaries
Join for life . . .
Ny Tearday

Mothers spiritual
Come to the life my sisters
+ take what you need
doesnt matter my brothers
Your sunday creed
Cause each one's a lover
to this winter nite star
a pilgram a pioneer
thats who you are
Feel this love my brothers + sisters
Feel the season turn
She is the mother of time

ocean   I   Rap song Intro   II

I want the roll (beat 2-3)
roll of the ocean   < not your lies)   R
I want the roll (beat other? drum?)   e
roll of the ocean   p
          sweet (not alibi?)   e
     sweet elemental soul is   a
I want it , (3x ?)   (bind's cry)   t   > start the
                                                               singing
I want the elemental roll   rushing   coming out
                             is not wise   of the talking
                                                               setting it
I dont want the Bomb   free
        ego pride
   the big erection
        in the sky   to people, to nature   to
                                      to music, to animals →   people
I want full fillment .   nature
                                      I want sweetness.   animals
I want Satisfaction   I want give sweet things)
                                      I want Sweet things   sweetness
I want sweet thing progress   I want It's sweet things
I want (I've got frustration)   I want to give

I want peace on earth
I want so many
              red
              rose
                yellow
                brown   I want
                orange/fire   I want to rebel
what do I care   east coast purple-leaved   I want to have fun
I'm an earth one /   Autumns left to live raise a bit of hell
 what can I do
  I'm an earth   what can I do
   angel /celestial angel   I'm an angel
                                               a woman
  Celestial woman/ earth woman   a deadly rebel

  an angel
  a woman < a bright one
  It's hell being human < It's hell
                          being
 (For a brilliant woman   in this
              her own   democratic
                            pile of crap

East coast

water
ocean
Progressive form
Closer working supports

WED:
TODAY

note) - Leave key for Ning
in mailbox →
PRACTICE
TOES
HAIR
COUNT BLESSINGS
Exercise / walk

* PRACTICE + pack

Call out
Hebrew Tutor
Jane Fonda } + MEDITATE
Darken Hair.
Count Blessings

(WALK ONCE
Headphones)

* COUNT BLESSINGS

* Darken Hair?
Sew blue skeet + wash
✓ Lipstick — redder (less blue)
Toe nails
Water Trees
Jeff - is there side entrance to divising
Maria - my Social security card room in chance
along with Jeff.
Roscoe - Russel at awards
Dave - alert band VH1 - doublecheck
call Back
CALL ART - $24 + shipping ? - ceiling
- smoke detect.
- WOLF ? windows
(next week
Make Key. Hebrew tee tutor in school
my checks) - George - pay Roscoe check on time

18 yrs ago today   I could say / would
The ad light faded from the sky / you asked y
Daddy (Father) lay your flowers do The (with y
sudden
let tears touch the ground   (with y
your   a rose + a tear   wet
may tears mixed with anger
    will be my healing
        18 yrs (later)
start dealing with the feeli

    as
    The universe unfa
    Your a father m
    To the festiv

18 yrs ago today
Light faded
You strod to the holy grass
(where) you lay your flowers
+ let your tears touch the g

So lay your flowers down
where your tears touch the ground

18 yrs ago today
Lights of my youth
Mom left so soo
You left so soo
Now I say/realize
stare

18 yrs ago today
~~The~~
Grandpa + I
    bid you find goodb
we were fools
    for pearls
but we tried
off to save the world
    each likes fa
The lights of eac
faded
So let me lac
    from the
    safety
    of the
    show
    to
    the
    hand
    se

When there's laughter all around me
And my family & friends surround me
If I seeem to forgetful-
Remind me

That

Somewhere in the world
People are weak
Be aware
And while you speak
your mind
Others can't speak
Be aware

And while your children
sleep
Somewhere in the world
A child is homeless
When we have so much
Should any child
be homeless Be Aware
No not even one child

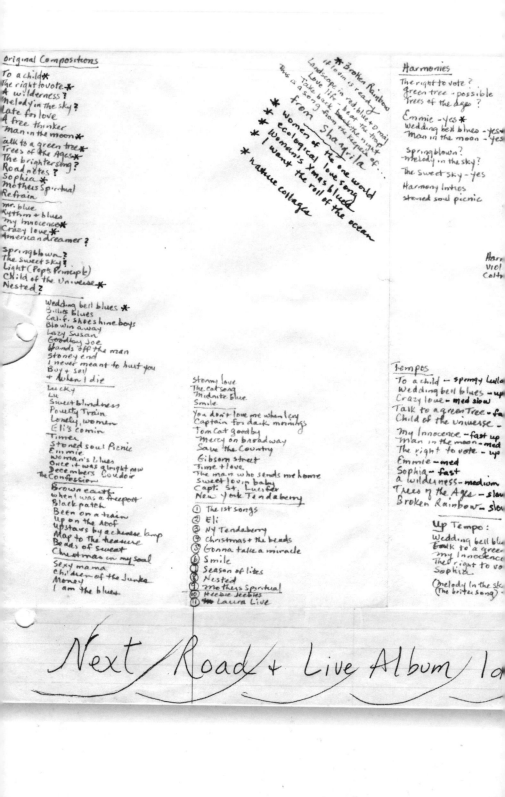

Original Compositions

To a child *
The right to vote *
A wilderness
Melody in the sky ?
Late for love
A free thinker
Man in the moon *
Talk to a green tree *
Trees of the Ages ?
The brighter song ?
Road notes ?
Sophia *
Mothers Spiritual
Refrain

Mr. blue
Rythm + blues
My Innocence *
Crazy love *
American dreamer ?

Springblown ?
The Sweet Sky ?
Light (Pop's Principle)
Child of the Universe *
Nested ?

Wedding bell blues *
Billies blues
Calif. shoeshine boys
Blowin away
Lazy Susan
Goodbye Joe
Hands off the man
Stoney end
I never meant to hurt you
Buy + sell
+ When I die

Lucky
Lu
Sweet blindness
Poverty Train
Lonely women
Eli's comin
Timer
Stoned soul Picnic
Emmie
Woman's blues
Once it was alright now
December's Boudoir
The Confession

Brown earth
When I was a freeport
Black patch
Been on a train
Up on the roof
Upstairs by a chinese lamp
Map to the treasure
Beads of sweet
Christmas in my soul
Sexy mama
Children of the Junks
Money
I am the blues

Broken Rainbow
It lo vin is ready
Landscape in red, blue + D mai
Love life - be at the front
Take back the night
This is a song from the keeper of...

from *Shangrila*

* Women of the one world
* ecological love song
* Woman's Xmas blues
* I want the roll of the ocean
* Nature collages

Stormy love
The cat song
Midnite blue
Smile
You don't love me when I cry
Captain for dark mornings
Tom Cat goodby
Mercy on broadway
Save the Country
Gibson street
Time + love
The man who sends me home
Sweet lovin baby
Capt. St. Lucifer
New York Tendaberry

① The 1st songs
② Eli
③ NY Tendaberry
④ Christmas + the beads
⑤ Gonna take a miracle
⑥ Smile
⑦ Season of lites
⑧ Nested
⑨ Mothers Spiritual
⑩ Heebie Jeebies
⑪ Laura Live

Harmonies

The right to vote ?
green tree - possible
Trees of the Ages ?

Emmie - yes *
Wedding bell blues - yes
man in the moon - yes

Springblown ?
Melody in the sky ?

The Sweet sky - yes

Harmony Intros
stoned soul picnic

Harm
Viol
Coll

Tempos

To a child — springy Lullab
Wedding bell blues — up
Crazy love - med slow
Talk to a green Tree - fa
Child of the universe -

My Innocence - fast up
Man in the moon - med
The right to vote - up
Emmie - med
Sophia - fast
a wilderness - medium
Trees of the Ages - slow
Broken Rainbow - slow

Up Tempo:
Wedding bell blue
Talk to a green
My Innocence
The right to vo
Sophia

(Melody In the sk
(The brites song)

Next Road + Live Album | a